MW01087170

ALLIS-CHALMERS

FARM TRACTORS
AND CRAWLERS

DATA BOOK
1914 to 1963

TERRY DEAN

First published in 2000 by MBI Publishing Company, PO Box 1,
729 Prospect Avenue, Osceola, WI 54020-0001 USA

MBI Publishing Company books are also available at discounts in bulk quantity
for industrial or sales-promotional use. For details write to Special Sales Manag-
er at Motorbooks International Wholesalers & Distributors, 729 Prospect
Avenue, PO Box 1, Osceola, WI 54020-0001 USA.

Library of Congress Cataloging-in-Publication Data Available
ISBN 0-7603-0770-9

On the front cover: Allis-Chalmers fans recognize the Model WC as one of
the most popular tractors of the 1930s and 1940s. Its successor, the Model
WD, with an engine nearly the same as the WC except for an increase in
rpm and carburetor size, was also a tremendous success. In 1950, A-C produced a staggering 36,870 WDs! This fine, restored 1951 WD, #95067 is
owned by Eric Onsrod, Janesville, WI. *Andrew Kraushaar*

On the back cover: The Allis-Chalmers Model U changed the industry in
1932. It was the first tractor equipped with pneumatic tires to be sold by a
manufacturer. By 1939, all of the major tractor companies were selling tires
as standard equipment.

Printed in the United States of America

Contents

Acknowledgments

Much help and cooperation from many sources were needed to put this book together. The patience and support of my editor, John Adams-Graf from MBI Publishing Company, always gave me the inspiration needed when tough spots came along.

Although this is an unofficial publication that is not connected to AGCO Corporation in any way, I wish to thank them. AGCO Corporation, a world leader in the manufacturing of farm equipment, has shown a sincere interest in the Allis-Chalmers roots of their own history. Permissions for the use of pictures in this book were kindly granted and greatly appreciated by this author.

I owe a big thanks to Alan King of King's Books of Ohio. Alan unselfishly allowed the use of photographs from his book, Allis-Chalmers 1918–1960: An Informal History.

I have enormous respect for Charles Wendel and Norm Swinford. They both researched the Allis-Chalmers' history in great depth with accuracy. These men rolled up their sleeves and performed the unimaginable task of finding the history of Allis-Chalmers equipment and organizing it into books.

Dave Bowers, Tom Copland, Ron Nelson, Bill Orr, Larry Renck, and Bob Thomasson all spent time gathering information on several models. To them, I am very grateful. Ron Nelson kindly researched several crawler models and never seemed to lose enthusiasm. Tom Copland from Edinburgh, Scotland, diligently researched details about the British ED-40 tractor. To Roger Culbert, who once ran an Allis-Chalmers dealership, I give special thanks for his help with several details. Also, I appreciate Nan Jones of The Old Allis News for her help with some hard-to-find details and contacts. As busy as she was, she patiently took the time to answer my questions.

The biggest thanks must go to my best friend, who is also my wife, Lana. She and our daughters, Kristy, Taron, and Maggie, always supported my effort to write this book. For several months they put up with a part-time husband and father as I researched and typed. I only hope I can support them as well when they take on projects that seem worthwhile to them.

Introduction

How to Use This Book

It's been a challenge to clearly present such a large amount of information in this pocket-sized book. By following these instructions, you will be able to completely understand all of the data.

Many tractor and crawler models changed throughout production, and the "Comments" section of the book will reflect many of these differences. On some models with major changes and corresponding Nebraska testing, there is more than one section of specifications.

The production total with each model heading reflects the total number of units built in that particular arrangement, not necessarily the total number of that particular model. In the listing, the grand total for that model will be compared to that particular arrangement. Further breakdowns of production will be found in the "Comments" or "Standard Features" listings near the end of each section. On tractor models with more than one section in this book, one must refer back to the first section for that model to find the beginning serial number for each year. These serial numbers will be listed under the heading "Production History."

One must be careful to understand and differentiate between a tractor serial number and engine number. This book has breakdowns for both. Locations of both serial and engine numbers are listed in the beginning of each model section. It is important to note that only the serial number can be used to date a tractor; engine numbers cannot.

The steel wheels and tire sizes of tractors use a different form of measurement. Steel wheel sizes are displayed with the outside diameter first, followed by the width. Solid rubber tires use the same rule. Pneumatic tires show the width first, followed by the rim diameter.

The tune-up section for each model lists a Champion spark plug. This book in no way is endorsing this specific product brand, but rather, uses this brand as a standard because it is one of the easiest brands to convert using spark plug charts. In most cases, the spark plugs listed are recommended for light workloads. This book is not intended to be a service directory, and therefore one should consult the proper manuals for more precise tune-up information.

The height of a tractor refers to the highest point, unless otherwise stated. The weight of the tractor is the Nebraska test weight without added ballast, unless otherwise stated.

In the crawler section, there is a category called "rollers per side." This refers only to the number of bottom track rollers on each side and not to any upper support rollers.

Glossary

BTDC: Before top dead center
Cane tractor: High-clearance tractor
Cowl: Rear-engine enclosure at dash
Distillate: One type of low-grade fuel
Drawbar (engine rating): Maximum horsepower measured by pull
GPM: Gallons per minute
Grouser: Standard type of crawler track shoe
Grove tractor: An orchard tractor, used around trees
I-head: Engine has valves in head (rocker-arms)
Industrial rear tires: Rear tires with wider and more massive cleats
L-head: Engine has valves in block (flathead)
Live axle: Axle is driven directly by tractor differential
Live hydraulics: Hydraulic pump is not interrupted by master clutch
Live PTO: PTO shaft not interrupted by master clutch
LPG: Liquefied petroleum gas
Maximum pull: Most pounds of draw possible
Orchard model: Tractor with special shielding for tree branches
Power-Director: A type of high- and low-speed range unit
Power-Shift rear wheels: Tread is adjusted using tractor power and
    angled rim rails
PTO: Power take-off
PTO/belt (engine rating): Maximum horsepower at PTO or belt pulley
Rear tread: Rear width of tractor measured from wheel centers
Rice tires: Rear tires with very deep and wide-spaced cleats
Road tractor: Designed for highway maintenance, heavier built wheels
Row-crop tractor: Tractor has adjustable tread and adequate clear-
    ance for straddling crop rows
rpm: Revolutions per minute
Shuttle clutch: Unit changes direction of tractor in all gears
Snap-Coupler: Quick-attach implement system
Timing: Ignition or injection timing (advance)
Track gauge: Width of crawler from center to center of tracks
Turf tires: Rear tires with low massive lugs (nonaggressive traction)
Wheatland: A type of fixed-tread tractor with wide tires and fenders
Wheelbase: Length of tractor from wheel centers

Although the Allis-Chalmers Model 10-18 was a sturdy machine, the fast-paced tractor industry ruthlessly antiquated this three-wheeler almost as soon as it was introduced. Less than 3,000 units were made between 1914 and 1923.

Allis-Chalmers Model 10-18

Nebraska test number	not tested
Serial numbers	not known
Location of serial number	left side of frame below radiator
Production years	1914–1923
Engine	Allis-Chalmers opposed two-cylinder L-head
Bore and stroke	5.25x7 inches
Rated rpm	720
Displacement	303 cubic inches
Fuel	
Run	kerosene
Start	gasoline
Engine ratings (factory)	
Drawbar	10 horsepower
Belt	18 horsepower
Maximum pull	1,650 pounds
Speed	
Forward gear	2.3 mph
Reverse	2.3 mph
Length	140 inches
Width	70 inches
Height	75 inches
Weight	4,800 pounds
Carburetor	Kingston Dual
Ignition (magneto)	K-W or Kingston
Air cleaner	Bennett (dry)
Front wheel	32x6 inches
Rear wheel	56x12 inches
Fuel tank capacity	20 gallons
Auxiliary fuel tank	5 gallons
Cooling capacity	6 gallons

Engine lubrication (not from sump)	Detroit Lubricator
Side dipper oil capacity	1 pint each
Transmission oil capacity	2 gallons (600w)
Tune-up	
Spark plug used	Champion W-14
Spark plug gap	0.025 inches
Ignition point gap	0.016 inches
Timing (advance)	10 to 15 degrees BTDC
Price	
Model 10-18	$1,950 in 1914
Model 10-18	$895 in 1920
Model 10-18 (clearance price)	$360 in 1923
Paint	

Tractor is painted dark green with red wheels plus yellow pin stripes and lettering

Options

Guiding device (a self-steering attachment that follows plow furrows)

Comments

Allis-Chalmers officially announced its first true production tractor, the Model 10-18, on November 15, 1914.

The Model 10-18 was built in an era that was infested with fierce competition. Sixty-one tractor companies manufactured about 21,900 tractors in 1915. In 1923, more than 100,000 Fordson tractors alone were built compared to only four Allis-Chalmers Model 10-18 tractors. Poor tractor sales eliminated most of the tractor companies during the 1920s, but Allis-Chalmers persisted as a gladiator in the "tractor wars." By the early 1930s, Allis-Chalmers was a major contender in the tractor sales market.

The 10-18 was a fine tractor in its day with two drive wheels and a massive cast-steel frame. Compared to other tractors of this era, the 10-18 was better than most in quality and design.

Only a handful of 10-18 tractors have survived.

Model 10-18 Standard Features

Tricycle wheel configuration (9-foot turning radius)
56x12-inch rear wheels (48 lugs and 24 spokes each wheel)
An 8-roller pinion drives each exposed final drive ring gear
Each final drive ring gear has eight sections (eight teeth each)
One-piece heat-treated steel frame with no rivets
Adjustable swivel drawbar (14-inch lateral adjustment)
25-inch crop clearance at the axle (14-inch at the oil pan)
14.5-inch diameter by 6.5-inch wide belt pulley (720 rpm)
Detroit lubricator
Expanding-shoe clutch (two shoes, Allis-Chalmers brand)
2.9375-inch diameter drive axles

Production History (10-18 model)

Year	Units produced
1914–1918	not known
1919	71
1920	31
1921	45
1922	38
1923	4

Allis-Chalmers Model 6-12
(total production approximately 1,471)

Nebraska test number	54
Serial numbers	not known
Location of serial number	brass plate on cast frame/fuel tank
Location of engine number	brass plate on left side of block
Production years	1919–1926
Total production	approx. 1,471
Engine	LeRoi Model 2C 4-cylinder L-head
Bore and stroke	3.125x4.5 inches
Rated rpm	1,200
Displacement	138 cubic inches
Fuel	gasoline
Engine ratings	
Drawbar	6.27 horsepower
Belt	12.37 horsepower
Maximum pull	1,142 pounds
Speed	
Forward gear	2.4 mph
Reverse	2.4 mph
Length	156 inches
Drive wheel tread	54 inches
Height	72 inches
Weight	2,500 pounds
Carburetor	Kingston Model L
Ignition (magneto)	Eisemann, Dixie, or Splitdorf
Air cleaner	Bennett (dry)
Front drive wheel (steel)	48x6 inches
Sulky wheel (steel)	28x6 inches
Fuel tank capacity	9.5 gallons
Cooling capacity	3.5 gallons
Crankcase oil capacity	1.125 gallons
Tune-up	
Firing order	1-3-4-2
Spark plug used	Champion W-14
Spark plug gap	0.025 inches
Ignition point gap	0.020 inches
Timing (static)	26 degrees BTDC
Price	
Model 6-12 General Purpose	$850 in 1920
Model 6-12 General Purpose (sellout)	$295 in 1923

Paint
The tractor is painted dark green with red wheels and yellow pin stripes.

Options
Foot-operated plow lift (powered by sulky wheel)
Road wheels (20 flat spokes each with thick rims)
Rubber lugs (80 each wheel)
Steel lugs

Drive wheel extension rims
Extended (wide) angle-iron cleats
Directed exhaust (dual-exhaust blows sand off final drive pinions)

Comments

The Model 6-12 General Purpose farm tractor has a 347-pound cast frame with a built-in fuel tank and pressed-in axles. This vertical frame also has a toolbox built into the right side. Each drive wheel weighs 212 pounds and has 20 round spokes and 10 gear segments that are driven by a pinion gear with five rollers.

The Model 6-12 General Purpose Farm Tractor was also made in a Model B version that was lower than the standard version. This model was advertised as an orchard tractor. The steering yoke was changed to raise the beam (pipe) almost level with the hood, and the drive wheel axles were higher on the frame. No production figures have been found to determine if the Model B was made in numbers of any extent. Pictures exist of an orchard version of the Model B with optional citrus fenders.

To operate the 6-12 tractor, a hand lever on the left disengages the clutch when pulled back. As this lever is pulled back all the way, the brake band tightens around a drum in the differential. The lever on the right side of the pipe is the shifter. Pushing forward makes the tractor go backward, and pulling the lever back will make it go forward. Neutral is in the middle. Rated speed in each direction is 2.4 miles per hour.

The 6-12 had a removable single (early type) or twin sulky wheel attachment. This sulky assembly was removed for use of attached-wheeled implements. The single sulky design apparently was changed to a twin style around 1920.

An adapter was sold called the Duplex Hitch that hooked two General Purpose models together. The engines faced away from each other, and the controls were interlocked to work these tractors as a single articulated four-wheel-drive unit.

Model 6-12 General Purpose Standard Features

Cast main frame
Front-wheel drive with articulated steering
48x6-inch steel drive wheels (20 angle-iron cleats each)
Thermosiphon cooling system
Allis-Chalmers brand differential and sliding-gear transmission
Borg and Beck dry plate clutch
Exposed final drive ring gears and roller pinion gears drive front wheels
10-inch diameter by 5.5-inch wide belt pulley (1,000 rpm)

Production History (6-12 model)

Year	Units produced
1919	303
1920	467*
1921	72*
1922	249*
1923	211*
1924	99
1925	62
1926	8

* Included in these totals are 20 cane models that were built in 1920, 6 in 1921, 6 in 1922, and 13 in 1923. No information has been found to include details about the cane or orchard versions.

Allis-Chalmers Models 15-30 and 18-30 (total production 1,161)

Nebraska test number	55
Serial numbers (all E models)	5000–25611
Serial numbers (15-30 and 18-30 models)	5000–6160
Location of serial number	top of transmission by shifter
Location of engine number	left side of block between inspection covers
Production years (all E models)	1918–1936
Production years (15-30 and 18-30 models)	1918–1921
Total production (all E models)	16,862
Total production (15-30 and 18-30 models)	1,161
Engine	Allis-Chalmers vertical four-cylinder
Bore and stroke	4.75x6.50 inches
Rated rpm	830
Displacement	460.7 cubic inches
Fuel	kerosene or gasoline
Engine ratings (kerosene)	
Drawbar	20.55 horsepower
Belt	33.41 horsepower
Maximum pull	3,500 pounds
Speed	
First gear	2.31 mph
Second gear	2.82 mph
Reverse	2.30 mph
Wheelbase	96 inches
Rear tread	66 inches
Height	68 inches
Weight	6,000 pounds
Carburetor	
Kerosene	Kingston E Dual
Gasoline	Kingston L
Ignition (magneto)	Dixie 46, K.W., or Eisemann
Air cleaner	Bennett (centrifugal) or Taco (water siphon)
Front wheel (steel)	36x6 inches
Rear wheel (steel)	50x12 inches
Fuel tank capacity (kerosene)	25 gallons
Starting fuel tank (gasoline)	7.75 gallons
Water (injection) tank capacity	7.75 gallons
Cooling capacity	10 gallons
Crankcase oil capacity	12 quarts
Transmission oil capacity	7 gallons
Tune-up	
Firing order	1-3-4-2
Spark plug used	Champion W-14
Spark plug gap	0.030 inches
Ignition point gap	0.020 inches

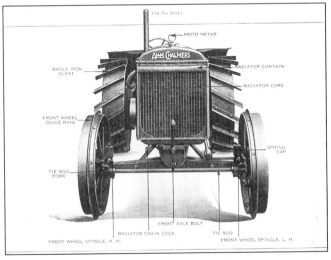

Cut No. 16515

MOTO METER

ALLIS CHALMERS

ANGLE IRON
CLEAT

RADIATOR CURTAIN

RADIATOR CORE

FRONT WHEEL
GUIDE RING

SPRING
CAP

TIE ROD
FORK

FRONT AXLE BOLT

RADIATOR DRAIN COCK

TIE ROD

FRONT WHEEL SPINDLE, R. H.

FRONT WHEEL SPINDLE, L. H.

As one of the finest quality tractors in its class, the Allis-Chalmers Model E 18-30 was not an inexpensive unit at $1,785 in 1920. During the 1920s, a new Fordson could be acquired for less than $500. Although sales of the Model E tractors were less than sensational during its 19-year lifespan, a steady number were built most years.

Timing (static)   26 degrees BTDC
Price $1,785 in 1920
Paint
The tractor is painted dark green with red wheels plus yellow pin stripes.

Options
Canvas canopy
Rubber street pads for rear wheels
Rear wheel extensions
Riding rims (road bands)
Canvas engine curtains
Motometer (radiator cap thermometer)

Comments
   The early 15-30 models had louvered engine covers, narrow fenders, and brass radiator tanks. By early 1919, the steel engine covers were eliminated, the fenders were full-width, and the radiators had cast-iron tanks.
   The first units made were designated as the Model 15-30 until early factory tests showed a more favorable horsepower rating. This justified renaming the tractor the Model 18-30 with no major changes. The Nebraska test no. 55 for kerosene that was completed in September 1920 showed an rpm of 830. When tested a year later on gasoline (test no. 83) in September 1921, the rated rpm was increased to 930 and the tractor put out 43.75 belt horsepower, but it wasn't until 1923 that the tractor was renamed the Model 20-35. The Models 15-30, 18-30, 20-35, and 25-40 were all versions referred to as the Model E. As the Model E increased in horsepower through the years, the model numbers eventually changed also.

Models 15-30 and 18-30 Standard Features
Full rear fenders and platform
Removable gray iron cylinder sleeves
Unit frame construction
50x12-inch rear steel wheels (18 cleats each, 18.5 inches long)
Expanding shoe hand-clutch
15-inch diameter by 7.5-inch wide belt pulley (830 rpm)

Production History (Models 15-30 and 18-30)

Year	Beginning Number
1918	5000
1919	5006
1920	5161
1921	6015
Ending serial number	6160

With an increase in horsepower, the Model E 20-35 engine ran 100 rpm faster than the older Model E 18-30. In 1927, the 20-35 was redesigned to lower the selling price.

Allis-Chalmers Model 20-35 (total production 14,276)

Nebraska test number	83
Serial numbers (all E models)	5000–25611
Serial numbers (20-35 models)	6161–24185
Location of serial number	top of transmission by shifter
Location of engine number	left side of block
Production years (all E models)	1918–1936
Production years (20-35 models)	1923–1930
Total production (all E models)	16,862
Total production (all 20-35 models)	14,276
Total production (20-35 long-fender)	1,909
Total production (20-35 short-fender)	12,367
Engine	Allis-Chalmers vertical two-cylinder I-head
Bore and stroke	4.75x6.5 inches
Rated rpm	930 rpm
Displacement	460.7 cubic inches
Compression ratio	5.2:1
Fuel	kerosene or gasoline
Engine ratings (gasoline)	
Drawbar	25.45 horsepower
Belt	43.73 horsepower
Maximum pull	3,510 pounds

Speed

First gear	2.58 mph
Second gear	3.16 mph
Reverse	3.16 mph

Length

Prior to serial number 8070	152.0 inches
Serial number 8070 and up	140.5 inches
Rear width (overall)	75 inches
Height (to top of steering wheel)	68 inches
Weight	6,640 pounds

Carburetor

Prior to serial number 9870	Wheeler-Schebler or Kingston L
Serial number 9870 and up	Zenith C6EV
Ignition (magneto)	Eisemann model GS4
Air cleaner	Allis-Chalmers centrifugal/oil-mesh

Front steel wheel (French and Hecht)	36x6 inches
Rear steel wheel (French and Hecht)	50x12 inches
Fuel tank capacity	32 gallons
Cooling capacity	10 gallons
Crankcase oil capacity	12 quarts
Transmission oil capacity	7 gallons

Tune-up

Firing order	1-3-4-2
Spark plug used	
Gasoline	Champion W-10
Distillate	Champion W-14
Spark plug gap	0.030 inches
Ignition point gap	0.015 inches
Timing (static)	26 degrees BTDC

Price

Model 20-35 Farm Tractor (long fender)	$1,685 in 1925
Model 20-35 Special Tractor	$1,885 in 1925
Model 20-35 Farm Tractor (short fender)	$1,295 in 1928
Model 20-35 Farm Tractor (short fender)	$1,205 in 1929

Paint

Prior to 1927	dark green with red wheels
1927 to 1929	dark green tractor and wheels
1929 and up	Persian Orange tractor and wheels

Options

Adjustable bow-top cab canopy or winter cab
PTO assembly with a clutch (542 rpm)
Electric lights
18.75x3.5-inch rear wheel cleats or rubber street pads
5- or 6-inch rear wheel spade lugs (24 each wheel)
Riding rims (road bands)
8-inch wide rear wheel extensions

Comments

The Model E tractor was referred to as the 18-30 until a little over a year after the favorable Nebraska test no. 83 in September 1921. The Model E was then renamed the 20-35. The rpm was raised to 930 from the previous 830 and gasoline was used instead of kerosene to get the increased horsepower from the older Model 18-30.

From 1925 to 1930, several E models were sold under the Greyhound name. The Banting Machine Company sold these tractors from Toledo, Ohio. The "Banting" name was cast into a plate at the rear of the gas tank, and the "Greyhound" name was on the upper radiator casting. The colors remained the same as Allis-Chalmers' models.

Model 20-35 tractors prior to 1926 had oil cups under the hood for rocker-arm lubrication, while the 1926 models had the cups protruding through the hood. The 1927 and later model rocker-arms were pressure lubricated by the oil pump with external tubing.

The 20-35 tractor was changed to save money in 1927, starting at serial number 8070. The rear fenders were shortened to about 10 inches above the rear axle instead of about 12 inches below the axle on previous models. The operator platform was made smaller and the hood was widened. The wheelbase was shorter. There was a redesigned clutch assembly. The wheels were painted green like the rest of the tractor.

Further changes began in 1928 at serial number 9870. The steering column and worm gear were changed as well as the dash, transmission case, and clutch. The fan assembly had tapered roller bearings to replace the straight type on previous models.

Again in 1928, at serial number 16436, new changes were made. The transmission case and high-speed gears were changed. The oil pump was a direct-drive type, eliminating an idler gear that was used on previous models. Other changes were made to the fan assembly, tie rod, differential, and fuel filter.

Model 20-35 Farm Tractor Standard Features

50x12-inch rear steel wheels (24 spokes and 5-inch lugs)
Fenders (16-inch wide) and platform
13-inch diameter by 8.5-inch wide belt pulley (930 rpm)
94 drop forged parts

Model 20-35 Special Tractor Standard Features

Same features as the standard farm model plus the following:
Introduced in 1924 for the custom threshing market
High-compression engine (approx. 10 more belt horsepower)
Adjustable bow-top cab canopy
Dash-mounted carburetor and governor adjustment
Fulton exhaust whistle

Model 20-35 Special Road Tractor Standard Features

Introduced in February 1922
50x12-inch rear steel wheels (half-inch thick rims with 36 spokes)
Rear wheel weights (clamps to spokes)
Weighted solid-disc front steel wheels
Adjustable bow-top canopy
Fenders and platform

Production History (Model 20-35)

Year	Beginning Number
1923	6161
1924	6397
1925	6755
1926	7369
1927 (short-fender version)	8070
1928	9870*
1929	16762*
1930	23252
Ending serial number	24185

* Serial numbers 10001–12000 and 20251–22000 were not used.

Allis-Chalmers Model 25-40 (total production 1,426)

Nebraska test number	193
Serial numbers (all E models)	5000–25611
Serial numbers (25-40 models)	24186–25611
Location of serial number	top of transmission by shifter
Location of engine number	left side of block
Production years (all E models)	1918–1936
Production years (25-40 models)	1930–1936
Total production (all E models)	16,862
Total production (25-40 models)	1,426
Engine	Allis-Chalmers vertical four-cylinder I-head
Bore and stroke	5.00x6.50 inches
Rated rpm	1,000
Displacement	511 cubic inches
Compression ratio	4.0:1, 4.4:1, 5.2:1, 5.8:1
Fuel	kerosene or gasoline
Engine ratings	
Drawbar	33.82 horsepower
Belt	47.00 horsepower
Maximum pull	4,133 pounds
Speed	
First gear	2.5 mph
Second gear	3.25 mph
Reverse	3.25 mph
Length	140.5 inches
Rear tread	70 inches
Height (to top of steering wheel)	68 inches
Weight	7,200 pounds
Carburetor	Zenith C6EV
Ignition (magneto)	Eisemann G4
Air cleaner	Donaldson (oil)
Front wheel (steel)	36x6 inches
Rear wheel (steel)	50x12 inches
Fuel tank capacity	28 gallons
Auxiliary fuel tank capacity	1 gallon

The Model "E"
Steel Wheels

In its final form, the Model E cranked out over 33 horsepower at the drawbar and 47 horsepower on the belt. Renamed the 25-40, this tractor eventually evolved into the Model A.

Cooling capacity	10 gallons
Crankcase oil capacity	14 quarts
Transmission oil capacity	7 gallons
Tune-up	
Firing order	1-3-4-2
Spark plug used	
Gasoline	Champion W-10
Distillate	Champion W-14
Spark plug gap	0.030 inches
Ignition point gap	0.015 inches
Timing	26 degrees BTDC
Price	
25-40 (steel wheels)	$1,000 in 1934
25-40 (rubber)	$1,425 in 1934
Paint	
Persian Orange tractor and wheels	

Options

Rear steel wheel extensions (8-inch wide with eight lugs each)
18.75x3.5-inch rear wheel cleats (16 each wheel)
6-inch rear wheel spade lugs (24 each wheel)
Riding rims (road bands)
12.75x28-inch rear tires or 7.50x18-inch front tires
36x5-inch front wheels with solid rubber tires
50x10-inch rear solid rubber tires (French and Hecht spoke wheels)
50x10-inch solid rubber tires on extension rims (French and Hecht)
PTO with a clutch (542 rpm)

Model 25-40

Electric lights with Bosch RE6-1700R1 generator (no battery type)
6-volt Auto-Lite ML4178 starter plus lights (battery type)
Choice of cylinder bore: 4.75, 5.00, or 5.25 inches
Rubber street pads

Comments

The governor, water pump, carburetor, and air cleaner were different on the short-fender Model 20-35 and Model 25-40. Other than minor changes, both models were much alike. The improved horsepower ratings on the Model 25-40 were from a cylinder bore and rpm increase.

The Model A replaced the 25-40 during 1936.

The Greyhound tractors sold by the Banting Machine Company from 1925 to 1930 were E models. In 1930, the "Greyhound" name in the top radiator tank casting was replaced by "The Banting Machine Co. Toledo Ohio."

Model 25-40 Standard Features

50x12-inch rear steel wheels with 5-inch lugs (24 each wheel)
36x6-inch front steel wheels
Fenders and platform
13-inch diameter by 8.5-inch wide belt pulley (1,000 rpm)
Muffler

Production History (Model 25-40)

Year	Beginning Number
1930	24186
1931	24843
1932	24972
1933	25024
1934	25062
1935	25309
1936	25582
Ending serial number	25611

The Model L tractor was referred to as the 12-20 until shortly after the Nebraska Test no. 82 in September 1921. Powered by a Midwest brand engine, the tractor was renamed the Model 15-25 with no major changes. As the little brother to the Model E, this model was intended for smaller farms.

Allis-Chalmers Model L, 12-20, 15-25 (total production 1,705)

Nebraska test number	82
Location of serial number	plate on rear fuel tank support
Location of engine number	left side of engine below no. 4 cylinder housing
Serial numbers	20001–21705
Production years	1920–1927
Total production (all L models)	1,705
Engine	Midwest vertical four-cylinder I-head
Bore and stroke	4.125x5.25 inches
Rated rpm	1,100
Displacement	280.6 cubic inches
Fuel	gasoline
Engine ratings	
Drawbar	21.42 horsepower
Belt	33.18 horsepower
Maximum pull	2,560 pounds
Speed	
Model L Farm tractor and Road tractor	
First gear	2.3 mph
Second gear	3.1 mph
Reverse	3.1 mph
Model L Orchard	
First gear	2.1 mph
Second gear	2.8 mph
Reverse	2.8 mph

Length	130.5 inches
Rear tread	54 inches
Height (to top of radiator)	63 inches
Weight	4,550 pounds
Carburetor	
Gasoline models	Kingston L or Wheeler-Schebler A
Kerosene models	Kingston E Dual
Ignition (magneto)	Dixie 46C
Air cleaner	Taco no. 2 (water type)
Front wheel (steel)	32x6 inches
Rear wheel (steel)	46x12 inches
Fuel tank capacity	20 gallons
Cooling capacity	6 gallons
Crankcase oil capacity	10 quarts (approx.)
Transmission oil capacity	19 quarts (approx.)
Tune-up	
Firing order	1-3-4-2
Spark plugs used	
Gasoline	Champion W-10
Distillate	Champion W-14
Spark plug gap	0.030 inches
Ignition point gap	0.020 inches
Timing	25 degrees BTDC
Price	
Model 15-25 Farm Tractor	$1,495 in 1921
Model 15-25 Farm Tractor	$1,310 in 1922
Model 15-25 Farm Tractor	$1,385 in 1925
Paint	
Dark green with red wheels	

Options
Kerosene manifold with Kingston E Dual carburetor
46x15-inch rear steel wheels
8-inch wide rear wheel extensions
32x4-inch front wheel rim extensions (road tractor only)
4x3.5 or 4x4.75-inch rear wheel spade lugs (32 each wheel)
3.5x22.75 or 3.5x27-inch rear wheel cleats (16 each wheel)
1.5 or 3.5-inch front steel wheel guide ring
4.25x8-inch drawbar extension plate (orchard model only)

Comments
    The Model L tractor was referred to as the 12-20 until shortly after the Nebras-ka Test no. 82 in September 1921. Because of the higher horsepower ratings, the tractor was renamed the Model 15-25 with no major changes.
    On engine numbers up to 11962, the Midwest engines were somewhat differ-ent than ones made later. The early engine had a 1.25-inch rear camshaft bearing, aluminum floating (detached) water pump, and a large magneto bracket with integrated crankcase oil fill assembly and chained cap. Engines above number 11962 had a 2.187-inch rear camshaft bearing, cast-iron flanged water pump, small magneto base, and an oil fill pipe in the crankcase with a spring-loaded cap.

Prior to 1922 serial number 20456, the steering box had a 4-inch worm gear and a 9-tooth segment gear. In 1922 at tractor serial number 20456 and up, the steering box was heavier with a longer 5.375-inch worm gear and a segment gear with 11 teeth. The sheet metal steering box cover was changed to cast iron.

Prior to 1924, some Model L tractors had cast-iron oil pans. Later models had stamped-steel oil pans. Allis-Chalmers, Huber, J. G. Brill, and the Waukesha Company continued to build the Midwest engine design after the Midwest Engine Company of Indianapolis discontinued operations in 1924.

Model L Farm Tractor Standard Features
Expanding-shoe hand-clutch
Single lever handbrake (7-inch drum)
46x12-inch rear steel wheels (16 spokes each wheel)
2.5x18.5-inch rear wheel cleats (16 each wheel)
32x6-inch front steel wheels with 2.5-inch guide ring
12.5-inch diameter by 6.6-inch wide belt pulley (817 rpm)
One-piece bull gear (71 teeth)
Tool kit (wrenches, pliers, hammer, cold chisel, and screw driver)

Model L Orchard Tractor Standard Features
Introduced in February of 1924
Individual rear foot–operated brakes
42x12-inch rear steel wheels (two braces each)
27.625x6-inch solid-disc, front steel wheels (3.5-inch guide ring)
Below-hood exhaust and air cleaner inlet
Citrus fenders

Model L Road Tractor Standard Features
Individual rear foot–operated brakes
46x15-inch heavy rear steel wheels (0.625-inch thick rims)
Rear wheels with 20 spokes (1.5-inch diameter spokes)
3.5x17-inch rear wheel cleats (15 each wheel)
Special wide rear fenders
32x6-inch front steel wheels
Pomona 610 air cleaner

Production History (all L tractor models)

Year	Beginning Number
1921	20001
1922	20335
1923	20498
1924	20906
1925	20996
1926	21371
1927	21682
Ending serial number	21705

First produced with a Continental engine, the Model U was used heavily in the industrial realm as well as on the farm. The hard-rubber tires were one of numerous wheel options offered on this versatile tractor.

Allis-Chalmers Model U, Continental Engine (total production 7,404)

Nebraska test number	170
Serial numbers (all U models)	1–23050 (approx.)
Serial numbers (U, Continental engine)	1–7404
Location of serial number	stamped into rear of differential housing
Location of engine number	right side of block
Production years (all U models)	1929–1952
Production years (U, Continental engine)	1929–1932
Total production (all U models)	approx. 20,400
Total production (U, Continental engine)	7,404
Engine	Continental S10 vertical, four-cylinder L-head
Bore and stroke	4.25x5.0 inches
Rated rpm	1,200
Displacement	283.7 cubic inches
Fuel	kerosene or gasoline
Engine ratings	
Drawbar	25.63 horsepower
PTO/belt	35.04 horsepower
Maximum pull	3,679.5 pounds
Speed	
First gear	2.33 mph
Second gear	3.33 mph

Third gear	5.0 mph
Fourth gear	10.75 mph
Reverse	2.69 mph
Length	118.875 inches
Rear tread	52 inches
Height (to top of steering wheel)	53.75 inches
Weight	4,821 pounds
Carburetor	Schebler HD or Kingston
Ignition (magneto)	Eisemann G4, Bosch, or Bendix Scintilla
Air cleaner	Donaldson centrifugal
Front wheel (steel)	28x6 inches
Rear wheel (steel)	42x11.125 inches
Fuel tank capacity	23 gallons
Cooling capacity	5 gallons
Crankcase oil capacity	12 quarts
Transmission oil capacity	12 gallons
Tune-up	
Firing order	1-3-4-2
Spark plug used	
Gasoline	Champion W-10
Distillate	Champion W-14
Spark plug gap	0.030 inches
Ignition point gap	0.015 inches
Timing (static)	center flywheel mark "SPARK" in timing mark opening, magneto should fire no. 1 cylinder on top of compression stroke
Price	$895 in 1929
Paint	Persian Orange

Options

3.5x3.5-inch rear wheel angle cleats (10 each wheel)
6-inch rear wheel lugs (20 each wheel)
Front wheel guide rings
Transport bands (road bands)
11.25x24-inch rear tires and 6.5x16-inch front tires (1932 and after)
Rear platform
Muffler
10-inch diameter by 7.5-inch wide belt pulley assembly with clutch
Belt roller assembly for front axle
Lighting equipment (battery type or Presto-Lite generator)
6-volt Auto-Lite MAB4003 starter and Guide brand lights
PTO assemblies (1,095-rpm side-mount or 530-rpm rear-mount)
Double PTO assembly (industrial option)
Gear ratio B (3.8- to 16.0-mph industrial option)
Gear ratio C (4.3- to18.5-mph industrial option)
1,800-rpm engine speed governor (industrial option)
Foot accelerator (industrial option)
18-inch rear wheel drum type brakes (industrial handbrake option)
Spring-mounted heavy-duty front axle (industrial option)
Industrial seat or spring seat

Comments

Allis-Chalmers made the "United" tractor for the United Tractor and Equipment Corporation, an association company that they were an important part of. With about 40 companies involved, this association needed an industrial tractor to replace the American Fordson that ceased production in 1928. The Allis-Chalmers tractor had the "United" name cast into the top tank of the radiator. The United venture failed, and by 1930, Allis-Chalmers produced the tractor with only its name on it and shortened the model designation to "U." The Model U continued as a popular agricultural and industrial tractor for several more years. The United tractor color, Persian Orange, was adopted for the entire Allis-Chalmers tractor line.

The early style Donaldson centrifugal-type air cleaner with a glass jar was used prior to 1930 serial number 5872. From serial number 5872 to 7404, the Donaldson air cleaner had a stack-mounted precleaner that replaced the centrifugal chamber and dust jar. A special Vortox oil-type air cleaner was available as an upgrade after the Continental Model U production had ended.

The 1929–1932 serial numbers 1 to 7404 had the Continental L-head, 4.25x5-inch engine. Later Model U tractors have an Allis-Chalmers I-head engine.

Industrial U serial numbers are interspersed with regular Model U serial numbers. Industrial production totals are unknown.

Regular Model U (Continental engine) Standard Features
Three-plow capacity
French and Hecht brand steel wheels
Fenders (10-inch wide)
10-inch diameter by 7.437-inch wide belt pulley (1,094 rpm)

Industrial Model IU (Continental engine) Standard Features
The Industrial versions of the Model U were numerous. Not unlike the Fordson tractor, many aftermarket accessories and conversions were used on the Model IU. Conversions such as graders, cranes, loaders, crawlers, locomotives, winches, and dirt-haulers were just some of the many configurations made. Below is a list of some of the more common versions of the Model IU.

Model IU-1
    Has steel wheels, 42x11.125-inch rear, and 28x6-inch front wheels
Model IU-2
    Has solid rubber tires, 40x5-inch rear, and 28x4-inch front tires
Model IU-5
    Has solid rubber tires, dual 40x5-inch rear, and 29x5-inch front tires
Model IU-6
    Same solid rubber tires as the IU-5, but with retractable rear cleats
Model IU-7
    Has solid rubber tires, 40x10-inch rear, and 29x5-inch front tires
Model IU-8
    Has solid rubber tires, 40x12-inch rear, and 29x5-inch front tires
Model IU-10
    Has solid rubber tires, 40x12-inch rear with 6-inch extensions
Model IU-11
    Has pneumatic tires, 8x40-inch rear, and 4x26-inch front tires

Model IU-34
   Has air-turf tires, 14x24-inch rear, and 7.50x16-inch front tires
Model IU-N
   44-inch rear width, 40x5-inch rear, and 24x3.5-inch front solid tires
Model GU
   Trackson brand crawler conversion, 3.5-mph maximum speed
Model LU
   Trackson brand crawler conversion, 9.5-mph maximum speed
Model HU
   Double front-mounted winch tractor

Orchard Model U (Continental engine) Standard Features
Low exhaust
Rear citrus fenders
Steel shields (disc type) enclose front steel wheel spokes
Lower steering column angle and low rear-mounted seat
Extended operator controls

Production History (all U models)

Year	Beginning number
1929	1
1930	1975
1931	6554
1932	7262
1933	7419
1934	7685
1935	8063
1936	9471
1937	12822
1938	14855
1939	15587
1940	16078
1941	16722
1942	17137
1943	17470
1944	17802
1945	not found
1946	not found
1947	20774*
1948	21022*
1949	22128*
1950	23029*
1951-1952	not found

*There is much confusion on serial numbers during these years as they may not have been consecutive; these numbers were published in early 1964.

Allis-Chalmers Model U, Allis-Chalmers Engine (total production approximately 13,000)

Nebraska test number	237
Serial numbers (all U models)	1–23050 (approx.)
Serial numbers (UM engine)	7405 and up
Location of serial number	stamped into rear of differential housing
Location of engine number	right side of block below oil fill
Production years (all U models)	1929–1952
Production years (U, Allis engine)	1932–1952
Total production (all U models)	approx. 20,400
Total production (U, Allis engine)	approx. 13,000
Engine	Allis-Chalmers vertical four-cylinder (built by Waukesha)
Bore and stroke	
Serial numbers 7405–9988	4.375x5.00 inches
Serial number 12001 and up	4.5x5.00 inches
Rated rpm	1,200
Displacement	
Serial numbers 7405–9988	300.7 cubic inches
Serial number 12001 and up	318 cubic inches
Compression ratio	4.2:1
Fuel	distillate or gasoline
Engine ratings (300.7 cubic inches, distillate fuel, on rubber)	
Drawbar	30.07 horsepower
Belt	34.02 horsepower
Maximum pull	2,452 pounds
Speed (on rubber)	
First gear	2.66 mph
Second gear	3.5 mph
Third gear	4.75 mph
Fourth gear	11.5 mph
Reverse	3.25 mph
Length	118.5 inches
Rear tread (rubber)	65 to 76 inches
Height (to top of steering wheel)	53.5 inches
Weight	5,140 pounds (rubber)
	5,030 pounds (steel)
Carburetor	Zenith K5
Ignition (magneto)	Bendix Scintilla C-4, Eisemann, or Fairbanks-Morse FMOR
Air cleaner	
Serial numbers 7405–13006	Vortox (oil)
Serial numbers 13007 and up	Donaldson (oil)
Front wheel	6.65x16 inches (rubber)
	24x5 inches (steel)
Rear wheel	
Tire size prior to serial no. 22084	11.25x28 inches
Tire size serial no. 22084 and up	13x28 inches
Steel wheel size	45x11

Fuel tank capacity	23 gallons
Auxiliary fuel tank capacity (starting)	1 gallon
Cooling capacity	6 gallons
Crankcase oil capacity	10 quarts
Transmission oil capacity	12 gallons
Tune-up	
Firing order	1-2-4-3
Spark plug used	
Gasoline	Champion W-10
Distillate	Champion W-14
Spark plug gap	0.035 inches
Ignition point gap	0.020 inches (Fairbanks)
Timing (static)	32 degrees BTDC (flywheel)
Price	
Model U (steel wheels)	$840 in 1934
Model U (rubber)	$1,050 in 1934
Model UO (orchard, steel wheels)	$930 in 1934
Paint	Persian Orange

Options
Winter cab or open canopy
3.5x3.5-inch rear steel wheel angle cleats (10 each wheel)
6-inch rear steel wheel lugs (20 each wheel)
Front steel wheel guide rings (2.5- or 3.5-inch)
Transport bands (half-section road bands)
11.25x24-inch rear rubber tires and 6.5x16-inch front rubber tires
150-pound weights for rear wheels with tires (third pair optional)
Rear platform
10-inch diameter by 7.5-inch wide belt pulley with clutch
Belt roller assembly for front axle
6-volt Auto-Lite MAB-046 starter
Guide brand lights (two headlights and one taillight)
PTO assembly with a clutch (530 rpm)
Muffler
Gear ratio B (3.8–16.0 mph industrial option)
Gear ratio C (4.3–18.0 mph industrial option)
1,800-rpm engine speed governor (industrial option)
Foot accelerator (industrial option)
18-inch drum-type rear brakes (industrial handbrake option)
Spring-mounted heavy-duty front axle (industrial option)
Engine side covers (industrial option)
Industrial seat

Comments
    The base-mount magneto was replaced by a flange-style at engine number 4587 and up.
    The shifting fork was not engaged into the fourth gear shifting collar groove on steel wheel models.
    With 1936 serial number 12001, the standard rear tire size was increased to 11.25x28 inches from the earlier 11.25x24 inches. The rear wheel style changed from spoke to cast

(excluding IU models). Beginning with serial number 22084 and up, the rear tire size was increased to 13x28 inches with wider rims.

Modified fenders and a high back seat were on all U models made at 1936 serial number 12001 and up.

The bore was increased from 4.375 to 4.5 inches, which in turn raised the displacement from 300.7 to 318 cubic inches at 1936 serial number 12001 and up.

The original steering gear was a Hannum brand, which changed to a Levine brand starting with Model U 1936 serial number 12401 and IU serial number 10002. The steering gear was changed again to a Ross brand at Model U 1937 serial number 13501 and up and Model IU serial number 10425 and up.

Prior to 1937 serial number 14120, front wheels with tires were the spoke style. At serial number 14120 and up, the wheels were a steel-disc type. The front-disc wheels and hubs changed from a six- to a five-bolt pattern starting at 1938 serial number 15314 and up.

Up to about 1960, Fred E. Cooper Inc. of Tulsa, Oklahoma, converted about 1,100 Allis-Chalmers tractors and power units into winch units for oil well maintenance. One version is mentioned here as it has the Model U serial numbers, but is actually more like the Model A. By putting the large Model E engine in the Model U drivetrain, you would have the basics for the original Model A. These units had a front frame extension with a pair of 5,000-foot winches mounted to it.

Model U (Allis-Chalmers engine) Standard Features
Unit frame construction
Foot-operated clutch
Fenders
10-inch diameter by 7.5-inch wide belt pulley (1,094 rpm)
150-pound weights for rear wheels with tires (two each wheel)

Model IU (Allis-Chalmers engine) Standard Features
Lower seat frame
Hand-operated clutch
Several versions available (see IU, Continental engine features)

Orchard Model U (Allis-Chalmers engine) Standard Features
Low exhaust
Rear citrus fenders
Steel shields (disc type) enclose the front steel wheels
Lower steering column angle and low rear-mounted seat
Extended operator controls

Allis-Chalmers Model UC, Continental Engine (total production 1,268)

Nebraska test number	189
Serial numbers (all UC models)	1–6217
Serial numbers (UC, Continental engine)	1–1268
Location of serial number	stamped into rear of differential housing
Location of engine number	right side of block
Production years (all UC models)	1930–1953
Production years (UC, Continental engine)	1930–1933
Total production (all UC models)	6,217
Total production (UC, Continental engine)	1,268
Engine	Continental S10 vertical four-cylinder L-head
Bore and stroke	4.25x5.0 inches
Rated rpm	1,200
Displacement	283.7 cubic inches
Fuel	kerosene or gasoline
Engine ratings	
Drawbar	24.98 horsepower
PTO/belt	36.09 horsepower
Maximum pull	3,763 pounds
Speed	
First gear	2.33 mph
Second gear	3.33 mph
Third gear	5.0 mph
Reverse	2.7 mph
Length	125.125 inches
Rear tread	69–80 inches
Height	67.625 inches
Weight	5,965 pounds
Carburetor	Schebler HD
Ignition (magneto)	Eisemann G4
Air cleaner	Donaldson centrifugal
Front wheel (steel)	24x5 inches
Rear wheel (steel)	42x2 inches
Fuel tank capacity	23 gallons
Auxiliary fuel tank capacity (starting)	1 gallon
Cooling capacity	5 gallons
Crankcase oil capacity	12 quarts
Transmission oil capacity	12 gallons
Final drive oil capacity (each)	2 quarts
Tune-up	
Firing order	1-3-4-2
Spark plug used	
Gasoline	Champion W-10
Distillate	Champion W-14
Spark plug gap	0.030 inches

Model UC, Continental Engine

Ignition point gap	0.015 inches
Timing (static)	Center flywheel mark "SPARK" in timing mark opening, magneto shouldfire no. 1 cylinder on compression stroke
Price	approx. $925 in 1933
Paint	Persian Orange

Options
Rear wheel spade lugs (18 each wheel)
6-inch rear steel wheel extensions (one or two used each side)
Half overtires (road bands)
11.25x24-inch rear tires and 6.5x16-inch front tires (1932 and up)
Special heavy-duty power lift
Combination PTO and power lift
10-inch diameter by 7.5-inch wide belt pulley with clutch (1,094 rpm)
Furrow guide (for plowing only)

Comments
    Serial number UC-1 through UC-31 had several differences from later models. These tractors had a fourth gear that would allow a 10-mile-per-hour speed. Later steel wheel models with the Continental engine came with no shifting fork, shaft, nor shifting collar for the fourth gear. The first 31 models also had different style rear wheels (same dimensions) and a lower steering gear ratio with a 15-tooth steering spindle gear compared to an 18-tooth gear on later models.

Model UC (Continental engine) Standard Features
Standard-duty power lift (mechanical)
Fenders
Individual 9-inch external band rear wheel handbrakes
42x2-inch rear steel wheels & 5.625x8-inch cleats (18 each wheel)
PTO assembly (530 rpm)
30-inch crop clearance under rear axle
10-inch diameter x 7.5-inch wide belt pulley (1,094 rpm)

Production History (all UC models)

Year	Beginning number
1930	1
1931	39
1932	1100
1933	1232
1934	1294
1935	1552
1936	2001
1937	2771
1938	3757
1939	4547
1940	4770

Model UC, Continental Engine

1941	4972
Ending regular UC serial number	5037
1942	none built
1943	none built
All UC tractors from 1944 and up are Cane units*	
1944	5038
1945	none built
1946	none built
1947	5068
1948	5268
1949	5526
1950	5644
1951	5806
1952	5939
1953	6143
Ending serial number	6217

*Cane production figures from Norm Swinford's *A Guide to Allis-Chalmers Farm Tractors*.

The New Model "UC"
Air Tires

With rubber tires, the Model UC was advertised to handle three 14-inch plows. The Allis-Chalmers engine bore was increased in 1936 at serial number 2282, and the tractor was restyled in 1937 at serial number 2819.

Allis-Chalmers Model UC, Allis-Chalmers Engine (total production 4,949)

Nebraska test number	238
Serial numbers (all UC models)	1–6217
Serial numbers (UC, Allis engine)	1269–6217
Location of serial number	stamped into rear of differential housing
Location of engine number	right side of block below oil fill
Production years (all UC models)	1930–1953
Production years (UC, Allis engine)	1933–1953
Total production (all UC models)	6,217
Total production (UC, Allis engine)	4,949
Engine	Allis-Chalmers vertical four-cylinder (built by Waukesha)
Bore and stroke	
Serial numbers 1269–2281	4.375x5.0 inches
Serial numbers 2282 and up	4.5x5.0 inches
Rated rpm	1,200
Displacement	
Serial numbers 1269–2281	300.7 cubic inches
Serial number 2282 and up	318 cubic inches
Compression ratio	4.2:1
Fuel	kerosene or gasoline

Engine ratings (rubber)
- Drawbar — 28.85 horsepower
- PTO/belt — 34.09 horsepower
- Maximum pull — 2,593 pounds

Speed (rubber tires)

Model UC
- First gear — 2.66 mph
- Second gear — 3.50 mph
- Third gear — 4.75 mph
- Fourth gear — 11.50 mph
- Reverse — 3.0 mph

Model UC (Cane)
- First gear — 3.28 mph
- Second gear — 4.26 mph
- Third gear — 5.92 mph
- Fourth gear — 13.98 mph
- Reverse — 3.74 mph

Length — 125.125 inches
Rear tread — 69–80 inches
Height — 66.375 inches
Weight — 6,115 pounds (rubber)
Carburetor — Zenith K-5
Ignition (magneto) — Bendix-Scintilla C-4 or Fairbanks-Morse

Air cleaner
- Serial numbers 1269–2818 — Vortox (oil)
- Serial number 2819 and up — Donaldson (oil)

Front wheel (steel) — 24x5 inches

Rear wheel
- Steel wheel (prior to serial number 2819) — 42x2 inches
- Steel wheel (serial number 2819 and up) — 45x2 inches

Fuel tank capacity — 24 gallons
Auxiliary fuel tank capacity (starting) — 1 gallon
Cooling capacity — 6 gallons
Crankcase oil capacity — 10 quarts
Transmission oil capacity — 12 gallons
Final drive oil capacity (each) — 2 quarts

Tune-up
- Firing order — 1-2-4-3
- Spark plug used
  - Gasoline — Champion W-10
  - Distillate — Champion W-14
- Spark plug gap — 0.035 inches
- Ignition point gap — 0.020 inches
- Timing (static) — 32 degrees BTDC (flywheel)

Price
- Model UC (steel wheels) — $940 in 1934
- Model UC (rubber) — $1,150 in 1934

Paint — Persian Orange

Options

Electric starter and lights available in 1939 and after
6-inch wide rear steel wheel extensions (one or two used each side)
Rear steel wheel spade lugs (18 each wheel)
11.25x28-, 12.75x28-, and 13.50x28-inch rear tires (serial no. 2819 and up)
Rear wheel weights
6.00x16-inch front tires
10-inch diameter by 7.5-inch wide belt pulley assembly (clutch type)
Standard power lift or special heavy-duty power lift
Combination PTO and power lift

Comments

The 1933 serial number 1269 was the first UC tractor to use an Allis-Chalmers Model UM engine.

At 1936 serial number 2282 and up, the UC had the engine bore increased from 4.375 inches to 4.50 inches; this increased the displacement from 300.7 cubic inches to 318 cubic inches.

The Model UC was restyled at 1937 serial number 2819 and up. Changes were made to the fuel tank, hood, fenders, platform, dash, and many other parts. The newer hood had sides that flared toward the radiator, while the fenders were shorter. Rear steel wheel size was increased from 42x2 inches to 45x2 inches, while the optional rear tire size was increased from 11.25x24 inches to 11.25x28 inches.

On early steel wheel Model UC tractors, serial numbers 1269 to 2818, the transmissions were built without fourth gear. On later steel wheel models, the shifting fork was not engaged into the fourth gear shifting collar groove; but the fourth gear was intact.

The front wheels and hubs were changed from a six-bolt to a five-bolt style at 1938 serial number 4337 and up.

About 1,150 units were made as Cane models from 1944 to 1953. Three hundred and sixty-one Cane models were made from 1937 to 1941, but these serial numbers are interspersed with regular UC models. The Thompson Machinery Company of Thibodaux, Louisiana, received most of the UC Cane tractors. After 1953, when the UC Cane production ended, Thompson purchased model UC parts from Allis-Chalmers and built its own Cane tractors. These Thompson Cane models include the UCD and the XTD models. These models were both powered by a General Motors two-cylinder diesel engine. The UCD looked somewhat like the UC Cane model and the XTD was a four-wheel-drive version of the UCD.

Model UC (Allis-Chalmers engine) Standard Features

42x2- or 45x2-inch rear steel wheels
5.625x8-inch rear wheel cleats (18 each wheel)
Fenders
Swinging drawbar (8.75-inch lateral adjustment)
Unit frame construction
10-inch diameter by 7.4375-inch wide belt pulley (1,094 rpm)
PTO assembly (530 rpm)

Model UC Cane (late) Standard Features

12x38-inch rear tires and 5.25x21-inch front tires
70–79.5-inch rear tread
25.5-inch crop clearance

As a manufacturer of some of the greatest prairie tractors ever built, Advance-Rumely Thresher Company tried to rescue its perishing company by entering the small tractor market with its DoAll. The DoAll was inherited by Allis-Chalmers after the company bought the subjugated Advance-Rumely in 1931. This little tractor was sold as a regular four-wheel unit or as a convertible model that could be changed to a front-wheel-drive cultivator tractor.

Rumely DoAll Tractor (total production 3,193 units)

Nebraska test number	154
Serial numbers	501–3693
Serial number location	on dash
Engine number location	right side of block near center
Production years	1928–1931
Total production	3,193
Engine	Waukesha vertical four-cylinder L-head
Bore and stroke	3.5x4.5 inches
Rated rpm	1,400
Displacement	173.2 cubic inches
Fuel	gasoline
Engine ratings	
Drawbar	16.32 horsepower
PTO/ belt	21.61 horsepower
Maximum pull	2,012 pounds
Speed	
First gear	2.625 mph
Second gear	3.75 mph
Reverse	2.875 mph

Wheelbase

Tractor version	60.4375 inches
Cultivator version	103.4375 inches
Length (tractor version)	108 inches

Rear tread

Nonconvertible version	46
Convertible version	60, 66, or 75 inches
Height (to top of exhaust)	64.75 inches
Height (to top of radiator)	59.25 inches
Weight	3,702 pounds
Carburetor	Stromberg MI or Zenith
Ignition (magneto)	Eisemann GV4
Air cleaner	Donaldson
Front steel wheel (tractor)	26x5 inches

Steel drive wheel

(French and Hecht)	42x7 inches
Castor wheel (cultivator)	25x5 inches
Fuel tank capacity	15.0 gallons
Cooling capacity	5.5 gallons
Crankcase oil capacity	4 quarts

Tune-up

Firing order	1-2-4-3
Spark plug used	Champion W-10
Spark plug gap	0.025 inches
Ignition point gap	0.015 inches
Price	$543 in 1931

Paint (controversial)

Prior to June 1931	Rumely Blue with red letters
June 1931 and after	Green with red letters

Options

66-inch wide front axle (used as a plow guide)
10-inch diameter by 5.5-inch wide belt pulley (800–1,400 rpm)
PTO assembly (538 rpm)
Angle-iron drive wheel cleats

Comments

On October 10, 1927, the Toro Manufacturing Company announced the sale of the rights to the Advance-Rumely Company for their combination tractor and cultivating machine. The resulting DoAll tractor was announced on April 13, 1928. The stockholders of the infirm Advance-Rumely Company voted on May 29, 1931, to sell the assets of their company to Allis-Chalmers. The final deal was arranged on June 1. The remaining DoAll tractors were assembled and sold as the Allis-Chalmers Rumely DoAll Tractor until at least 1932.

The DoAll was available in a 46-inch tread, nonconvertible unit or in the wider treads as a convertible cultivating unit. The cultivator unit was converted by turning the final drive units forward and removing the front axle; then a castor wheel assembly was added to support the rear of the unit. The seat, steering wheel, and operator controls were extended rearward, so that the cultivators would be mounted near the operator's feet. A bolt-on narrow front axle for dual wheels was another, but less popular, version available.

Rumely DoAll (Straight Four-Wheeled) Standard Features
Rear wheel fenders
42x7-inch steel drive wheels (French and Hecht brand)
2.5-inch spade lugs (24 each wheel) and road bands
32.5-inch crop clearance
Twin-Disc brand hand-clutch

Rumely DoAll (Convertible to Cultivator) Standard Features
Rear sulky and operator extension kit
42x7-inch steel drive wheels (French and Hecht brand)
Final drives rotate to change wheelbase
Twin-Disc brand hand-clutch

Production History (DoAll Models)

Year	Beginning number
1928	501
1929	701
1930	2116
1931	3514
Ending serial number	3693

Rumely Model 6A (total production 802)

Nebraska test number	185
Serial numbers	501–1,302
Location of serial number	plate on cowl
Location of engine number	on gear cover at front of engine
Production years	1930–1931
Total production	802
Engine	Waukesha vertical six-cylinder L-head
Bore and stroke	4.25x4.75 inches
Rated rpm	1,365
Displacement	404 cubic inches
Compression ratio	5.38:1
Fuel	gasoline
Engine ratings	
Drawbar	33.57 horsepower
PTO/belt	48.37 horsepower
Maximum pull	4,273 pounds
Speed	
First gear	2.82 mph
Second gear	3.66 mph
Third gear	4.72 mph
Reverse	3.44 mph
Length	163 inches
Rear width	70 inches
Height	74 inches
Weight	6,370 pounds
Carburetor	Zenith 156
Ignition (magneto)	American Bosch U6
Air cleaner	Vortox
Front wheel (steel)	30x6 inches

Rear wheels (steel)	48x12 inches
Fuel tank capacity	25 gallons
Cooling capacity	9 gallons
Tune-up	
Firing order	1-5-3-6-2-4
Spark plug used	Champion W-10
Spark plug gap	0.025 inches
Ignition point gap	0.016 inches
Timing	18 degrees BTDC
Price (old stock)	
Rumely 6A (steel wheels)	$1,100 in 1934
Rumely 6A (rubber tires)	$1,395 in 1934
Paint	

The tractor is dark green with red letters and has stripes on the flat spokes of the models with steel wheels. There is a double red pinstripe on each fender near the outer edge. Rumely-6 diamond transfers are used on the fenders facing the rear near seat height.

Options
12.75x28-inch rear and 7.50x18-inch front tires
6-inch, rear-wheel spade cleats (uses 28 on standard wheel)
Heavy-duty steel drive wheels (uses 32 cleats each)
2-inch high by 6-inch wide angle iron cleats (14 each wheel)
7-inch drive wheel extensions (uses 14 angle-iron cleats each)
Front wheel extensions (4 inches wide)
Front hitch or road bands (rear wheel)
Lights (one front plus one rear)
Electric starting, lighting, and ignition equipment
50x10-inch rear and 29x5-inch front wheels with solid rubber tires
50x10-inch rear wheel extensions for solid rubber tires
Radiator guard, screen, or curtain
Scrapers for drive wheels and extensions
PTO assembly (785–892 rpm)

Comments
   Allis-Chalmers sold the Rumely 6A until at least 1935, even though almost all of the production occurred in 1931.
   The Rumely Six was advertised to have six forward speeds, but it had only a three-speed transmission with the engine operating at a choice of two governed speeds of 1,200 and 1,365 rpm.

Rumely 6A Standard Features
48x12-inch rear steel wheels
4.75-inch spade cleats (28 each wheel)
Adjustable drawbar
13-inch diameter by 8-inch wide belt pulley (785–892 rpm)
Drive wheel fenders and platform

Production History (Rumely 6A)

Year	Beginning number
1930	501
1931	503
Ending serial number	1302

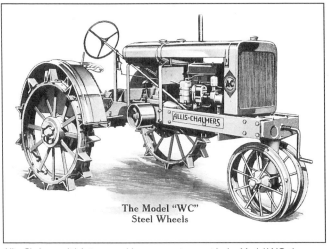

The Model "WC"
Steel Wheels

Allis-Chalmers didn't just stumble upon a winner with the Model WC; the company knew what the average farmer wanted and they built it. A perky two-plow tractor with no fat, the WC was a real hit on the small farms. With more than 178,000 units produced in its 16 years on the market, this was a lot of tractor for the money. This version is the nonstreamlined Model WC.

Allis-Chalmers Model WC (nonstreamlined) (total production 74,329)

Nebraska test number	304
Serial numbers (all WC models)	1–178202
Serial numbers (nonstreamlined WC)	1–74329
Location of serial number	stamped into rear of differential housing
Location of engine number	rear side of block
Production years (all WC models)	1933–1948
Production years (nonstreamlined WC)	1933–1938
Total production (all WC models)	178,202
Total production (nonstreamlined WC)	74,329
Engine	Allis-Chalmers vertical four-cylinder I-head
Bore and stroke	4.0x4.0 inches
Rated rpm	1,300
Displacement	201 cubic inches
Compression ratio	5.5:1
Fuel	distillate or gasoline
Engine ratings (gasoline, rubber tires)	
Drawbar	24.16 horsepower
PTO/belt	29.93 horsepower
Maximum pull	3,136 pounds

Speed	
First gear	2.5 mph
Second gear	3.5 mph
Third gear	4.75 mph
Fourth gear	9.25 mph
Reverse	2.0 mph
Length	136 inches
Rear tread	65 to 76 inches
Height	63 inches
Weight	3,310 pounds (rubber)
Carburetor	Kingston or Zenith 0–7078
Ignition (magneto)	
Prior to engine number W-3522	Bendix-Scintilla C-4
Engine number W-3522 and after	Fairbanks-Morse FMJ4B3 or FMJ4B3A
Air cleaner	United
Front tire (dual, narrow axle)	
Prior to serial number 23529	5.25x17 inches
Serial number 23529 and up	5.5x16 inches
Rear tire	11.25x24 inches
Fuel tank capacity	15 gallons
Auxiliary fuel tank capacity (starting)	1 gallon
Cooling capacity	4 gallons
Crankcase oil capacity	6 quarts
Transmission oil capacity	1 gallon
Final drive oil capacity (each)	0.5 quarts
Tune-up	
Firing order	1-2-4-3
Spark plug used (gasoline)	
Prior to 1938 engine no. 289000	Champion W-10
1938 engine no. 289000 and up	Champion J-8C
Spark plug gap	0.035 inches
Ignition point gap	0.020 inches (Fairbanks)
Timing (static)	30 degrees BTDC (flywheel)
Price	
Model WC (steel wheels)	$675 in 1934
Model WC (rubber)	$825 in 1934
Paint	Persian Orange

Options

40x6-inch rear steel wheels with 5-inch spade lugs (20 each wheel)
5-inch wheel extensions for 40-inch steel wheels (10 lugs each)
40x2-inch skeleton style rear steel wheels (18 spade lugs each)
24x4-inch front steel wheels for dual, narrow front axle
Rear tire sizes, 9.00x28, 7.50x36, and 9.00x36 inches offered
Single front wheel with a 9.00x10-inch tire
Wide front axle with 6.00x16-inch tires or 28x6-inch steel wheels
Cane version (high-crop)
Inner or outer rear wheel weights (150 pounds each)
PTO assembly (534 rpm)
Power lift assembly
Tire chains

Comments

The 1933 serial numbers prior to 29 have four-cylinder Waukesha L-head engines with a 3.625x4.5-inch bore and stroke and a 186-cubic inch displacement.

The WC was advertised as the Model W All-Crop until the first part of 1934.

The base-mount magneto was changed to a flange-mount at engine number 3522 and up.

Optional PTO drive units on WC models prior to 1935 are driven from the belt pulley access on the right side of the tractor. WC tractors made in 1935 and after have the PTO drive unit driven by the transmission from the underside.

Engine crankpin diameter was 1.9995 inches until 1935 serial number 3665. The size was increased to 2.3745 inches.

Front wheels are a nonreversible, 17-inch spoke type prior to 1936, serial number 23529. The wheels are reversible, 16-inch disc style at serial number 23529 and afterwards.

Front wheels and hubs are integrated prior to serial number 23529. Serial numbers 23529–59627 have six lugs on separate wheels and hubs. The 1937 serial number 59628 and up have five lugs.

Rear wheels for 24-inch tires are the spoke type prior to 1937 serial number 59636. Serial number 59636 and up have disc wheels.

A one-piece starting crank for the standard model with dual front wheels was used prior to 1938 serial number 68611. At serial number 68611 and up an extension stayed on the tractor and the crank was removable.

Model WC (nonstreamlined) Standard Features

Narrow front axle with dual wheels (8-foot turning radius)
Platform and full-width fenders
Rubber tires
26-inch crop clearance under rear axle
Sliding-gear, four-speed transmission
Individual rear handbrakes
Swinging drawbar (10.5-inch lateral adjustment)
9-inch diameter by 6.5-inch wide belt pulley and drive (1,170 rpm)

Production History (all WC models)

Year	Beginning number
1933	1
1934	29
1935	3127
1936	13870
1937	31784
1938	60790
1939	75216
1940	91534
1941	103517
1942	114534
1943	123171
1944	127642
1945	134624
1946	148091
1947	152845
1948	170174
Ending serial number	178202

Allis-Chalmers Model WC (streamlined)
(total production 103,873)

Nebraska test number	not tested
Serial numbers (all WC models)	1–178202
Serial numbers (streamlined WC)	74330–178202
Location of serial number	stamped into rear of differential housing
Location of engine number	left side of block, rear of carburetor
Production years (all WC models)	1933–1948
Production years (streamlined WC)	1938–1948
Total production (all WC models)	178,202
Total production (streamlined WC)	103,873
Engine	Allis-Chalmers vertical four-cylinder I-head
Bore and stroke	4.0x4.0 inches
Rated rpm	1,300
Displacement	201 cubic inches
Compression ratio	5.5:1
Fuel	distillate or gasoline
Engine ratings (from test no. 304)	
Drawbar	24.16 horsepower
PTO/belt	29.93 horsepower
Maximum pull	3,136 pounds
Speed	
First gear	2.5 mph
Second gear	3.5 mph
Third gear	4.75 mph
Fourth gear	9.0 mph
Reverse	2.0 mph
Length	136 inches
Rear tread	65–76 inches
Height (to top of steering wheel)	68 inches
Weight (shipping)	3,300 pounds (rubber)
Carburetor	Marvel-Schebler TSX159 or Zenith 161X7
Ignition (magneto)	Fairbanks-Morse FMJ4B3 or FMJ4B3A
Air cleaner	United (oil)
Front tire (dual, narrow axle)	5.50x16 inches
Rear tire	
Serial numbers prior to 81757	11.25x24 inches
Serial numbers 81757 and after	11x28 inches
Fuel tank capacity	15 gallons
Auxiliary fuel tank capacity (starting)	1 gallon
Cooling capacity	4 gallons
Crankcase oil capacity	6 quarts
Transmission oil capacity	1 gallon
Final drive oil capacity (each)	0.5 quarts

Tune-up
    Firing order   1-2-4-3
    Spark plug used (gasoline)   Champion J-8C
    Spark plug gap   0.035 inches
    Ignition point gap   0.020 inches
    Timing (static)   30 degrees BTDC (flywheel)
Price
    Model WC
      (rubber tires, lights, starter) $1,290 in 1947
    Model WC
      (on steel, no lights or starter) $998 in 1947
Paint   Persian Orange

Options
40x6-inch rear steel wheels with 5-inch spade lugs (20 each wheel)
6-inch wheel extensions for 40-inch steel wheels (10 lugs each)
40x2-inch skeleton style rear steel wheels (18 lugs each wheel)
24x4-inch front steel wheels for dual, tricycle front axle
Rear tire sizes, 9.00x28, 7.50x36, and 9.00x36 inches offered
PTO assembly (534 rpm)
9-inch diameter x 6.5-inch wide belt pulley and drive (1,170 rpm)
Live power lift assembly
Single front wheel with a 9.00x10-inch tire
Wide front axle with 6.00x16-inch tires or 28x6-inch steel wheels
Adjustable wide front axle (1947 to 1948)
Rear wheel weights

Comments
The streamlined WC was basically the same machine as the earlier exposed radiator models except for the following:
• Rounded end gas tank
• Mesh front grille
• Hood with tapered sides and horizontal ribs
• Smaller "clamshell" fenders
• Electric starter and lights as standard equipment

    The cylinder head was changed to a heavier type at engine number 289000 and up.
    During World War II, many WC models had the differential housing with a pressed-steel rear cover and bull gear housings that bolted onto the center casting to replace the one-piece casting on normal models. Starting at approximately serial number 132,005, this cost-saving option had an "S" suffix after the serial number.
    Engine numbers followed by a "G" are designed for gasoline only. Engine numbers followed by a "K" are designed to burn low-grade fuel or gasoline. When using a low-grade fuel, the manifold cover marked "K" must be used. The cover marked "G" should be used for gasoline only.
    Starting in 1938 until 1941, Allis-Chalmers made 411 WC Speed Maintainer graders from WC chassis. This road grader had a single front wheel and belly-mount blade. An improved W Speed Patrol grader was made from the WC chassis from 1940 to 1950. This grader had a wide front axle extended forward of the tractor with a belly-mount blade. The company built 3,751 W Speed Patrol units.

Model WF (nonstreamlined)

Model WC (streamlined) Standard Features
Rubber tires and clamshell fenders
6-volt Delco-Remy 1107006, 1107017, or Auto-Lite MAW4030 starter
Guide brand lights
Sliding-gear, four-speed transmission
Individual rear handbrakes
Swinging drawbar (10.5-inch lateral adjustment)

Allis-Chalmers Model WF (nonstreamlined) (total production 1,900)

Nebraska test number	not tested
Serial numbers (all WF models)	4–8353
Serial numbers (nonstreamlined WF)	4–1903
Location of serial number	stamped into rear of differential housing
Location of engine number	left or rear side of block
Production years (all WF models)	1937–1951
Production years (nonstreamlined WF)	1937–1940
Total production (all WF models)	8,350
Total production (nonstreamlined WF)	1,900
Engine	Allis-Chalmers vertical four-cylinder
Bore and stroke	4x4 inches
Rated rpm	1,300
Displacement	201 cubic inches
Compression ratio	5.5:1
Fuel	distillate or gasoline
Engine ratings (factory)	
Drawbar	20.41 horsepower
PTO/belt	25.45 horsepower
Maximum pull	3,054 pounds
Speed	
First gear	2.67 mph
Second gear	3.75 mph
Third gear	5.0 mph
Fourth gear	9.75 mph
Reverse	2.25 mph
Length	122 inches
Rear tread	46 to 57 inches
Height (to top of hood)	54.5 inches
Weight	3,490 pounds (rubber)
Carburetor	Zenith 124.5
Ignition (magneto)	Fairbanks-Morse FMJ4B3 or FMJ4B3A
Air cleaner	United (oil)
Front tire	5.5x16 inches

Model WF (nonstreamlined)

Rear tire	11.25x24 inches
Fuel tank capacity	15 gallons
Auxiliary fuel tank capacity	
(starting)	1 gallon
Cooling capacity	4 gallons
Crankcase oil capacity	6 quarts
Transmission oil capacity	1 gallon
Final drive oil capacity (each)	0.75 quarts
Tune-up	
Firing order	1-2-4-3
Spark plug used (gasoline)	
Before 1938 engine no. 289000	Champion W-10
1938 engine no. 289000 and up	Champion CJ-8
Spark plug gap	0.035 inches
Ignition point gap	0.020 inches (Fairbanks)
Timing (static)	30 degrees BTDC (flywheel)
Paint	Persian Orange

Options
40x6-inch rear steel wheels with 5-inch spade lugs (20 each wheel)
6-inch wheel extensions for 40-inch steel wheels (10 lugs each)
40x2-inch skeleton style rear steel wheels (18 spade lugs each)
24x4-inch front steel wheels
Rear tire sizes, 9.00x28, 7.50x36, and 9.00x36 inches offered
PTO assembly (534 rpm)
9-inch diameter x 6.5-inch wide belt pulley (1,170 rpm)
Radiator core guard screen
Muffler

Comments
Serial numbers 4-1903 were not streamlined and had full fenders and an exposed radiator shell.
The WF was based on the WC model, but had the final drive bull gears forward of the drive pinion. This made the WF lower and with a wheelbase about 17 inches shorter than the Model WC.
Rear wheels for 24-inch tires are a spoke-type prior to serial number 204. From serial number 204-1903, the rear wheels were a disc-type. All industrial WF models (also called Model IW) with tires had 24-inch disc-style wheels.

Model WF (nonstreamlined) Standard Features
Fenders
Individual rear handbrakes
Swinging drawbar (10.25-inch lateral adjustment)
Four-speed, sliding-gear transmission
Nonadjustable wide front end (11-inch clearance)
Bordered Allis-Chalmers transfer on frame rail sides (blue)

Model WF Orchard (nonstreamlined) Standard Features
Full citrus fenders
Lower steering shaft angle
Grille screen

Stub air cleaner tube with protective scoop
Bordered Allis-Chalmers transfer on hood sides (blue)

Production History (all WF models)

Year	Beginning number
1937	4
1938	389
1939	1336
1940	1892
1941	2300
1942	2704
1943	none built
1944	3004
1945	3195
1946	3510
1947	3748
1948	4111
1949	5500
1950	7318
1951	8316
Ending serial number	8353

Allis-Chalmers Model WF (streamlined) (total production 6,450)

Nebraska test number	not tested
Serial numbers (all WF models)	4–8353
Serial numbers (streamlined WF)	1904–8353
Location of serial number	stamped into rear of differential housing
Location of engine number	left side of block, rear of carburetor
Production years (all WF models)	1937–1951
Production years (streamlined WF)	1940–1951
Total production (all WF models)	8,350
Total production (streamlined WF)	6,450
Engine	Allis-Chalmers vertical, four-cylinder I-head
Bore and stroke	4.0x4.0 inches
Rated rpm	1,300
Displacement	201 cubic inches
Compression ratio	5.5:1
Fuel	distillate or gasoline
Engine ratings (advertised)	
Drawbar	24.16 horsepower
PTO/belt	29.93 horsepower
Maximum pull	3,136 pounds
Speed	
First gear	2.67 mph
Second gear	3.75 mph

Third gear	5.0 mph
Fourth gear	9.75 mph
Reverse	2.25 mph
Length	122 inches
Rear tread	46 to 57 inches
Height (to top of hood)	approx. 55 inches
Weight	3,490 pounds (rubber)
Carburetor	Zenith 161X7
Ignition (magneto)	Fairbanks-Morse FM4B
Air cleaner	United (oil)
Front tire	5.5x16 inches
Rear tire	11x28 inches
Fuel tank capacity	15 gallons
Auxiliary fuel tank capacity	
(starting)	1 gallon
Cooling capacity	4 gallons
Crankcase oil capacity	6 quarts
Transmission oil capacity	1 gallon
Final drive oil capacity (each)	0.75 quarts
Tune-up	
Firing order	1-2-4-3
Spark plug used (gasoline)	Champion CJ-8
Spark plug gap	0.035 inches
Ignition point gap	0.020 inches (Fairbanks)
Timing (static)	30 degrees BTDC (flywheel)
Price	
Model WF	
(rubber tires, starter, lights)	$1,340 in 1951
Model WF	
(steel wheels, no S&L)	$1,100 in 1951
Paint	Persian Orange

Options

40x6-inch rear steel wheels with 5-inch spade lugs (20 each wheel)
6-inch wheel extensions for 40-inch steel wheels (10 lugs each)
40x2-inch skeleton style rear steel wheels (18 lugs each wheel)
24x4-inch front steel wheels
Rear tire sizes, 9.00x28, 7.50x36, & 9.00x36 inches offered
PTO assembly (534 rpm)
9-inch diameter x 6.5-inch wide belt pulley (1,170 rpm)

Comments

The streamlined WF was basically the same tractor as the earlier exposed radiator models except for the following:
• Rounded end gas tank
• Radiator fully covered with rounded grille
• Hood with tapered sides and horizontal ribs
• Rear tire size increase to 11x28 from the earlier 11.5x24 inches
• Smaller "clamshell" fenders
    Serial numbers prior to 2304 used a canvas radiator screen for manual temperature control, and 1941 serial number 2304 until engine number 98778 used shutters.

Front wheels were made by the French and Hecht Company.

From 1948 to 1950, the Tractomotive Company built 202 Model TL-W loaders. These loaders were built on the Allis-Chalmers WF chassis and had the shovel behind the rear wheels and the operator controls reversed.

Model WF (streamlined) Standard Features
Fenders
11x28-inch rear tires and 5.5x16-inch front tires
6-volt Delco-Remy starter and Guide brand lights
Sliding-gear, four-speed transmission
Individual rear handbrakes
Swinging drawbar (10.25-inch lateral adjustment)
Rockford clutch and Perfex radiator

Allis-Chalmers Model TW "Speed Ace" (total production 87)

Nebraska test number	not tested
Serial numbers	1 to 87
Location of serial number	rib on right rear side of transmission case near top and dash
Location of engine number	left side of block
Location of wagon serial number	right side of wagon near bottom front
Production years	1935 to 1937
Total production	87
Engine	Allis-Chalmers vertical, four-cylinder I-head
Bore and stroke	5.25x6.5 inches
Rated rpm	1,050
Displacement	563 cubic inches
Compression ratio	5.2:1
Fuel	gasoline
Engine ratings	not tested
Speed	
First gear	4.0 mph
Second gear	6.75 mph (approx.)
Third gear	8.5 mph (approx.)
Fourth gear	16 mph
Reverse	5 mph
Weight	19,000 pounds with wagon
Carburetor	Zenith
Ignition	Fairbanks-Morse
Air cleaner	Vortox
Front tire	9.0x24 inches
Rear tire	18.00x24 inches
Fuel tank capacity	34 gallons
Cooling capacity	10 gallons
Crankcase oil capacity	14 quarts
Transmission oil capacity	5.5 gallons

Model TW "Speed Ace"

Tune-up
  Firing order   1-3-4-2
  Spark plug used   Champion W-14
  Spark plug gap   0.030 inches
  Ignition point gap   0.020 inches
  Timing (static)   26 degrees BTDC
Paint   Persian Orange

Options
Front grille guard

Comments
   In 1935, the Model TW was called the Speedster and in the following two years of production was called the Speed Ace.
   The Model TW (Tractor-Wagon) was built on a Model K crawler chassis. This industrial tractor was sold with a fifth wheel, bottom dump trailer with a 7.5-yard dirt capacity.

Model TW Standard Feature
7.5-yard capacity trailer
Four-speed transmission
Steering clutches allowing a 24-foot turning circle

Production History (TW Model)

Year	Beginning number
1935	1
1936	11
1937	38
Ending serial number	87

The Model A was an improved version of the older Model E. With more speed and horsepower, the Model A was quite a machine. Apparently the market for this type of tractor was ending, as sales were meager.

Allis-Chalmers Model A (total production 1,225)

Nebraska test number	not tested
Serial numbers	25701–26925
Location of serial number	top of transmission by shifter
Location of engine number	left side of block
Production years	1936–1942
Total production	1,225
Engine	Allis-Chalmers vertical 4-cylinder
Bore and stroke	
Gasoline	4.75x6.5 inches
Distillate	5.00x6.5 inches
Rated rpm	1,000
Displacement	
Gasoline	460.70 cubic inches
Distillate	510.50 cubic inches
Compression ratio	
Gasoline	4.4:1 or 5.25:1
Distillate	4.0:1
Engine ratings (factory ratings)	
Drawbar	39.7 horsepower
PTO/belt	51.2 horsepower
Speed	
First gear	2.5 mph
Second gear	3.75 mph
Third gear	5.0 mph
Fourth gear	9.0 mph
Reverse	3.0 mph
Length	138 inches

Rear tread	62.625 inches
Height (to top of hood)	60 inches
Weight	7,120 pounds
Carburetor	Zenith
Ignition (magneto)	Fairbanks-Morse or Splitdorf
Air cleaner	Vortox
Front tire	7.50x18 inches
Rear tire	13.50x28 inches
Fuel tank capacity	28 gallons
Auxiliary fuel tank capacity (starting)	1 gallon
Cooling capacity	11.5 gallons
Crankcase oil capacity	14 quarts
Transmission oil capacity	12 gallons
Tune-up	
Firing order	1-3-4-2
Spark plug used (gasoline)	Champion W-14
Spark plug gap	0.030 inches
Ignition point gap	
Fairbanks-Morse magneto	0.020 inches
Splitdorf magneto	0.015 inches
Timing (static)	26 degrees BTDC (flywheel)
Price	$1,495 in 1941
Paint	

The tractor is painted Persian Orange. The wheels of some of the early models with tires were black and later were orange. The rear rims are a silver color. Blue Allis-Chalmers hood transfers are used. A clutch lubrication instruction transfer is used on top of the transmission case at serial number 26682 and up.

Options
48x12-inch rear steel wheels with 5-inch spade lugs (24 per wheel)
Industrial steering gear assembly
6-volt Auto-Lite ML4178 or ML4214 starter
PTO assembly (531 rpm)

Comments
    Front wheels for tires were changed to a different rim clamp style on Model A tractors built after 1938 serial number 26525, and the transmissions were changed with a different shifting pattern. The early style transmission used the same case, shifting assembly, and many internal parts as the popular Model U tractor. The differential case and assembly was the same as the standard width Model U. The engine was from the earlier Model 25-40.
    At engine number 49763 and up, the cylinder head had 0.5-inch valve stems to replace the 0.4375-inch stems on previous models.
    Engine numbers followed by "K" are designed for low-grade fuel. Engine numbers followed by "G" are designed for gasoline.

Model A Standard Features
Fenders
Rubber tires
13-inch diameter by 8.5-inch wide belt pulley (948 rpm)
Swinging drawbar (17.5-inch lateral adjustment)

Model A Industrial Standard Features
Steering column is 9.3125 inches shorter than the farm version
Rubber tires
Rear wheel weights
Swinging drawbar (17.5-inch lateral adjustment)

Production History (A Model)

Year	Beginning number
1936	25701
1937	25726
1938	26305
1939	26614
1940	26782
1941	26896
1942	26915
Ending serial number	26925

ALLIS-CHALMERS MODEL B

The one-plow Model B was one of Allis-Chalmers foremost achievements. The success of this tractor carried Allis-Chalmers into numerous versions and models based on the same tractor. Hitting the market at less than $500 with rubber tires and a modern look, the Model B seemed to be just what the small farms needed.

Allis-Chalmers Model B, BE Engine (total production 61,300)

Nebraska test number	302
Serial numbers (all B models)	1–127461
Serial numbers (BE engine models)	101–61400
Location of serial number	top of transmission by shifter
Location of engine number	left or rear side of block
Production years (all B models)	1937–1957
Production years (BE engine models)	1938–1942
Total production (all B farm models)	118,101
Total production (BE engine models)	61,300
Engine	Allis-Chalmers vertical, four-cylinder I-head
Bore and stroke	3.25x3.5 inches
Rated rpm	1,400
Displacement	116 cubic inches
Compression ratio	4.67:1 or 4.92:1
Fuel	distillate or gasoline
Engine ratings (distillate fuel and rubber tires)	
Drawbar	12.97 horsepower
PTO/belt	15.68 horsepower
Maximum pull	1,473 pounds
Speed (on rubber)	
First gear	2.5 mph
Second gear	4.0 mph
Third gear	7.75 mph
Reverse	2.875 mph
Length	111 inches
Rear tread	40.5–52.5 inches
Height	62 inches
Weight (shipping)	1,900 pounds
Carburetor	Zenith 61AJ7 or Marvel-Schebler TSX-305
Ignition (magneto)	Fairbanks-Morse FR4B
Air cleaner	Donaldson (oil)
Front wheel	
Steel	22x4 inches
Tires	5.00x15 inches
Rear wheel	
Steel	36x6 inches
Tires	8x24 inches
Fuel tank capacity	13 gallons
Auxiliary fuel tank capacity (starting)	1 gallon
Cooling capacity	2 gallons
Crankcase oil capacity	4 quarts
Transmission/differential oil capacity	6 quarts

Model B, BE Engine

With belt pulley/PTO assembly	add one quart
Final drive oil capacity (each)	0.75 quarts
Tune-up	
Firing order	1-2-4-3
Spark plug used (gasoline)	Champion CJ-8
Spark plug gap	0.030 inches
Ignition point gap	0.020 inches (Fairbanks)
Timing (static)	30 degrees BTDC (flywheel)
Price	$518 in 1940 (rubber)
Paint	

Tractor and wheels are Persian Orange and hood transfers are blue. Model designation transfers for grille sides were not used until about 1953.

Options
Steel wheels (18 lugs on each wheel)
7x24-, 7.50x24-, 9x24-, or 10x24-inch rear tires
Rear steel wheel extensions and wider fenders
560-rpm PTO assembly (includes belt pulley drive)
8-inch diameter x 5.5-inch wide belt pulley (1,054 rpm)
Hydraulic lift system
Rear wheel weights (137 pounds each)
Side weights (96 pounds each)
6-volt starter and lights
Arched 38-, 43-, and 48-inch adjustable wide front axle (pre-1940)
Arched 50-, 55-, and 60-inch adjustable wide front axle (pre-1940)
Straight 38- to 60-inch adjustable wide front axle (1940-1941)
Straight 40.75- to 64.75-inch adjustable wide front axle (1942 and after)

Comments
Model B tractors with serial numbers prior to number 101 had a Waukesha L-head engine with a 113-cubic inch displacement and a rated rpm of 1,800. The Waukesha Bs had six-bolt front wheels, and many parts were not the same as later models. These exclusive parts included the radiator, grille, hood, fuel tank, torque tube, steering gear, and air cleaner to name a few.

The Model B came in variations of an Industrial, Asparagus Special, and Potato Special. These models have serial numbers that are interspersed with the regular Model B, except for the IB (industrial), which retained its own serial numbers after 1945.

Model B serial numbers 1–4380 had a welded-steel clutch pedal; all others had cast clutch pedals.

Model B tractors at 1939 serial number 12585 and up were available with special dished rear wheel centers for optional rear tread of 40 to 60 inches, 48 to 60 inches, or 40 to 68 inches.

The first IB was serial number 31101 manufactured in 1939.

On Model B tractors with manual heat control, beginning with serial number 43301 and IB serial number 55301, the canvas radiator curtain was replaced by a Hardy brand shutter assembly. The model B with the Waukesha engine had no curtain or shutter. A water manifold with a thermostat was used on BE engine number 23815 and up.

Model B tractors with engine numbers prior to 43896 and IB tractors prior to 1941 serial number 55301 had a vertical exhaust pipe with no muffler. Later

BE engine models used an underhood muffler with a vertical pipe. IB tractors prior to serial number 55301 had an option of a downward exhaust system with a muffler mounted under the tractor.

Optional adjustable wide front axles were arched before 1940. They were straight with a longer spindle drop on 1940 and later models. The arched style was offered in two widths: a narrow and a wide version, each with three width adjustments (see options). Tie rods of different lengths were used at various width settings.

Model B tractors prior to 1941 serial number 52718 and IB tractors prior to IB1001 have individual rear handbrakes; all others have foot-operated brakes.

A "C" channel frame surrounds the front half of IB tractors after 1946 serial number 1001 and was used to mount industrial equipment. This frame was optional on pre-1946 models.

The 32.375-inch-long torque tube on IB models was about 8 inches shorter than the standard Model Bs 40.4375-inch-long torque tube. The bull gear housings on the IB were turned forward to locate the bull gear in front of the drive pinion instead of below, as on standard Model B tractors. This lowered the height and shortened the wheelbase another 8 inches.

Regular Model B (BE Engine) Standard Features
Fenders
8x24-inch rear tires and 5.00x15-inch front tires
Solid arched nonadjustable wide axle
Swinging drawbar (22.25-inch lateral adjustment)

Industrial IB Standard Features
Total production (all engines) was about 2,850 units
A 2x5-inch "C" channel frame (optional before 1946)
7.5x24-inch industrial, four-ply rear tires
5.00x15-inch four-ply front tires
Low, nonadjustable wide front axle (2.5x1.75-inch solid steel)
Parking handbrake (pedal-type used prior to serial no. 1001)
Foot throttle (overrides standard throttle lever)
Spring-mounted pan type seat
(Coil spring used prior to serial no. 1001 and leaf-type afterwards)

Asparagus Special Standard Features
8x38-inch rear tires with special fenders
Adjustable arched wide front axle
High vertical drop front spindle assemblies
Rear tread of 41–52 inches
Crop clearance of 28 inches

Potato Special Standard Features
7x28-inch rear tires on special inset rims and special fenders
Adjustable wide front axle
Rear tread of 36 to 56 inches

Production History (all B models except IB models after 1945)
About 500 cane-type models and 13,100 adjustable, wide-front axle models were built in 1947 and after.

Model B, CE Engine

Year	Beginning number
1937	1
1938	97
1939	11800
1940	33502
1941	49721
1942	56782
1943	64501
1944	65502
1945	70210
1946	72265
1947	73370
1948	80556
1949	92295
1950	102393
1951	114527
1952	118674
1953	122310
1954	124201
1955	124711
1956	126497
1957	127186
Ending serial number	127461

Production History (Industrial IB models)
From 1939 to 1945, IB serial numbers were interspersed with regular Model B serial numbers. According to C. H. Wendel's *The Allis-Chalmers Story*, 260 IB units were made in this era.

Year	Beginning number
1946	1001
1947	1003
1948	1010
1949	1282
1950	1556
1951	1879
1952	2219
1953	2570
1954-1958	unknown

It is evident that approximately 1,023 units were made from 1953 to 1958.

Allis-Chalmers Model B, CE Engine (total production 56,961)

Nebraska test number	439
Serial numbers (all B models)	1–127461
Serial numbers (CE engine models)	64501–127461
Location of serial number	top of transmission by shifter
Location of engine number	rear or left side of block
Production years (all B models)	1937–1957
Production years (CE engine models)	1943–1957
Total production (all B farm models)	118,101
Total production (CE engine models)	56,961

Model B, CE Engine

Engine	Allis-Chalmers vertical four-cylinder I-head
Bore and stroke	3.375x3.50 inches
Rated rpm	1,500
Displacement	125.3 cubic inches
Compression ratio	4.7:1, 5.2:1, 5.75:1
Fuel	distillate or gasoline
Engine ratings (gasoline and rubber tires)	
Drawbar	19.51 horsepower
PTO/belt	22.25 horsepower
Maximum pull	2,667 pounds
Speed	
First gear	2.75 mph
Second gear	4.5 mph
Third gear	8.0 mph
Reverse	3.0 mph
Length	110.25 inches
Rear tread	40.5–52.5 inches
Height	76.75 inches
Weight	2,251 pounds
Carburetor	
Distillate	Zenith 219430
Gasoline	Zenith 216937, 212844, or Marvel-Schebler TSX-305
Ignition	
Magneto	Fairbanks-Morse FMJ4B3 or FMK4B3
Distributor (serial no. 123996 and up)	Delco-Remy 1111735
Air cleaner	Donaldson (oil)
Front wheel	
Steel	22x4 inches
Tires	4x15 inches
Rear wheel	
Steel	36x6 inches
Tires	9x24 inches
Fuel tank capacity	13 gallons
Auxiliary fuel tank capacity (starting)	1 gallon
Cooling capacity	2 gallons
Crankcase oil capacity	4 quarts
Transmission oil capacity	6 quarts
With belt pulley/ PTO assembly	add one quart
Final drive oil capacity (each)	0.75 quarts
Tune-up	
Firing order	1-2-4-3
Spark plug used (gasoline)	Champion CJ-8
Spark plug gap	0.032 inches
Ignition point gap	0.020 inches
Timing (static)	30 degrees BTDC (flywheel)

Price

Model B (rubber tires)	$1,130 in 1955
Model IB (rubber tires)	$1,570 in 1955

Paint

Tractor and wheels are Persian Orange and the hood transfers are blue, until 1948, then they are black. The air filter oil level transfers are not used after 1948. Model designation transfers for grille sides are used at about 1953 and after.

Options

Steel wheels and rear wheel extensions
600-rpm PTO assembly (includes belt pulley drive)
8-inch diameter by 5.5-inch wide belt pulley (1,129 rpm)
Hydraulic lift system (3,200-pound relief piston pump)
Rear wheel weights (100 or 142 pounds each)
Side weights (96 pounds each)
Adjustable wide front axle (40.75–64.75-inch tread)
8x24- or 10x24-inch rear tires
Larger 5.00x15- or 6.00x16-inch front tires (serial no. 26525 and up)
Side-hill hitch or Snap-Coupler (about 1954 and after)

Comments

The improved Model B had the new CE engine in the regular version as well as the industrial IB, Potato Special, and the Asparagus Special. The wheel configurations were the same on these models as the BE engine models.

A Zenith 216937 carburetor was used prior to CE engine number 4661.

In 1940 and after, a more substantial plate-steel PTO guard with a warning transfer replaced the sleeve-type guard that had no transfer.

Two thousand Model B tractors without wheels were sent to England in 1947 to 1949. British-made wheels and tires were added after arrival.

Model B 1942–1943 serial numbers 58401–65501 with steel wheels had a 20.5-inch air cleaner stack with an extra support bracket in lieu of the 12-inch stack on regular Model B tractors. The steel wheel models also used special rear fenders.

Model B 1953 serial number 123996 and up and IB serial number 2836 and up had the distributor ignition as standard equipment.

The Tractomotive Company built 69 rear-facing TL-B loader tractors based on the Model B chassis from 1948 to 1950.

Regular Model B Standard Features

Rubber tires plus rear fenders
Arched wide front axle
Swinging drawbar (22.25-inch lateral adjustment)
Delco-Remy 1107043, 1107096, or Auto-Lite MAW4031 starter
Guide brand lights (6-volt electrical system)

Asparagus, Potato, and Industrial Model Standard Features

See listings under "Model B, BE engine" Standard Features

By placing an engine from the Model B onto the chassis of the larger Model WC, the Model RC was born. The tractor was built for three years, and sales were mediocre at best. Allis-Chalmers was creative with existing inventories and offered many tractor variations with a minimum of retooling.

Allis-Chalmers Model RC (total production 5,501)

Nebraska test number	316
Serial numbers	4–5504
Location of serial number	stamped into rear of differential housing
Location of engine number	rear of block
Production years	1939–1941
Total production	5,501
Engine	Allis-Chalmers vertical, four-cylinder I-head
Bore and stroke	3.375x3.50 inches
Rated rpm	1,500
Displacement	125.3 cubic inches
Compression ratio	5.75:1
Fuel	distillate or gasoline
Engine ratings (distillate)	
Drawbar	15.25 horsepower
PTO/ belt	18.21 horsepower
Maximum pull	2,840 pounds
Speed	
First gear	2.0 mph
Second gear	2.8 mph
Third gear	3.75 mph
Fourth gear	7.5 mph
Reverse	1.75 mph
Length	136 inches
Rear tread	60.125–80.125 inches
Height (to top of steering wheel)	68 inches

Weight	4,005 pounds
Carburetor	Zenith 161J7
Ignition	Fairbanks-Morse FM43
Air cleaner	Donaldson (oil)
Front wheel	
Steel	24x4 inches
Tires	4.75x15 inches
Rear wheel	
Steel	40x6 inches
Tires	10x28 inches
Fuel tank capacity	12 gallons
Auxiliary fuel tank capacity	
(starting)	1 gallon
Cooling capacity	2 gallons
Crankcase oil capacity	4 quarts
Transmission oil capacity	4 quarts
Final drive oil capacity (each)	0.5 quarts
Tune-up	
Firing order	1-2-4-3
Spark plug used (gasoline)	Champion CJ-8
Spark plug gap	0.030 inches
Ignition point gap	0.020 inches
Timing (static)	30 degrees BTDC (flywheel)
Price	$785 in 1940 (rubber)
Paint	

Tractor and wheels are Persian Orange and the hood transfers are blue. No model designation transfer is used.

Options
9.0x28-inch rear tires
40x2-inch rear steel skeleton wheels
Front and rear wheel weights
8.0-inch diameter by 5.5-inch wide belt pulley assembly (1,350 rpm)
PTO assembly (532 rpm)

Comments
The Model RC was basically a WC streamlined tractor with the smaller CE engine, as is used in the Model B tractor.
Engines equipped to burn distillate as well as gasoline have the letter "K" after the engine number. Gasoline-only engines have the letter "G" after the engine number.

Model RC Standard Features
Four-speed transmission
Rubber tires plus rear fenders
Swinging drawbar (10.5-inch lateral adjustment)

Production History (RC models)

Year	Beginning number
1939	4
1940	4392
1941	5417
Ending serial number	5504

Allis-Chalmers Model C (total production 84,030)

Nebraska test number	363 and 364
Serial numbers	1–84030
Location of serial number	top of transmission by shifter
Location of engine number	left or rear side of block
Production years	1940–1950
Total production	84,030
Engine	Allis-Chalmers vertical, 4-cylinder I-head
Bore and stroke	3.375x3.50 inches
Rated rpm	1,500
Displacement	125.3 cubic inches
Compression ratio	4.75:1 (distillate)
	5.75:1 (gasoline)
Fuel	distillate or gasoline
Engine ratings (gasoline)	
Drawbar	18.43 horsepower
PTO/ belt	23.30 horsepower
Maximum pull	2,352 pounds
Speed	
First gear	2.5 mph
Second gear	3.75 mph
Third gear	7.5 mph
Reverse	2.75 mph
Length	110.25 inches
Rear tread	52–80 inches
Height (to top of muffler)	76.75 inches
Weight	2,200 pounds
Carburetor	
Distillate	Zenith 219430
Gasoline	Zenith 216937, 212844, or
	Marvel-Schebler TSX-305
Ignition (magneto)	Fairbanks-Morse FM-J4B
Air cleaner	Donaldson (oil)
Front wheel	22x4 inch (steel)
	4.00x15 inch (rubber)
Rear wheel	36x6 inch (steel)
	9x24 inch (rubber)
Fuel tank capacity	12 gallons
Auxiliary fuel tank capacity	
(starting)	1 gallon
Cooling capacity	2 gallons
Crankcase oil capacity	4 quarts
Transmission oil capacity	6 quarts
with belt pulley/ PTO assembly	add one quart
Final drive oil capacity (each)	0.75 quarts
Tune-up	
Firing order	1-2-4-3
Spark plug used (gasoline)	Champion CJ-8
Spark plug gap	0.032 inches
Ignition point gap	0.020 inches
Timing (static)	30 degrees BTDC (flywheel)

Model C

Price
Model C (dual narrow front axle)	$1,180 in 1950
Model C (adjustable wide front axle)	$1,260 in 1950
Model C (single front tire)	$1,205 in 1950

Paint

Tractor and wheel centers are Persian Orange and the rear rims are silver. Allis-Chalmers hood transfers have blue letters prior to 1948 and black letters in 1948 and after. No model designation transfer is used on the grille sides.

Options

600-rpm PTO assembly (includes belt pulley drive)
8-inch diameter by 5.5-inch wide belt pulley (1,129 rpm)
Hydraulic lift assembly
Front wheel weights (77 pounds each)
Rear wheel weights (100 pounds each)
Side weights (96 pounds each)
Swinging drawbar
Side-hill hitch for swinging drawbar
Single front wheel (6.00x12 inches)
Adjustable wide front axle
Cane option (high-clearance)

Comments

The Model C was a two-plow version of the one-plow Model B and came standard with a tricycle front axle with dual front wheels.

Production totals from Norm Swinford's *Allis-Chalmers Farm Equipment 1914–1985* show that there were 664 Model C tractors made with the single front wheel, 5,149 made with an adjustable wide front axle, and 20 Cane models.

A Zenith 216937 carburetor was used prior to engine number 4661. A Zenith 212844 or Marvel-Schebler TSX-305 carburetor was used afterward.

Model C serial numbers 1 to 5755 had individual handbrakes and all later models had individual foot-operated brakes.

The 1942 to 1945 Model C serial numbers 15714 to 32680 with steel wheels used a 22-inch air cleaner stack instead of the standard 12-inch stack.

Model C Standard Features

Two-plow capacity
Rubber tires plus rear fenders
Narrow front axle with dual front wheels
6-volt electric starter and lights

Production History (all C models)

Year	Beginning number
1940	1
1941	112
1942	12389
1943	18782
1944	23908
1945	30695
1946	36378
1947	39168
1948	51515
1949	68281
1950	80518
Ending serial number	84030

TRACTOR *FORESIGHT*

REAR ENGINE PERMITS STRAIGHT-AHEAD VISION

As the smallest Allis-Chalmers tractor built in its day, the garden or truck farmers cherished this unique Model G tractor. The N-62 Continental engine gave this tractor only 9 drawbar horsepower. The unobstructed view allowed the farmer to cultivate around crops with the utmost precision.

Allis-Chalmers Model G (total production 29,971)

Nebraska test number	398
Serial numbers	6–29976
Location of serial number	top of transmission by shifter
Location of engine number	left side of block on rear flange for starter
Production years	1948–1955
Total production	29,971
Engine	Continental AN-62 vertical, four-cylinder L-head
Bore and stroke	2.375x3.50 inches
Rated rpm	1,800
Displacement	62.0 cubic inches
Compression ratio	5.4:1 or 6.5:1
Fuel	gasoline or distillate
Engine ratings	
Drawbar	9.04 horsepower
PTO/belt	10.33 horsepower
Maximum pull	1,167 pounds
Speed	
Slow gear (option)	1.6 mph
First gear	2.25 mph
Second gear	3.5 mph
Third gear	7.0 mph

Reverse	2.0 mph
Length	114.50 inches
Wheel tread (front and rear)	36 to 64 inches
Height (to top of steering wheel)	55.69 inches
Weight	1,549 pounds
Carburetor	Marvel-Schebler TSV-13
Ignition	
Distributor	Delco-Remy 1111708
Magneto	Fairbanks-Morse
Air cleaner	Donaldson
Front tire	4.00x12 inches
Rear tire	6x30 inches
Fuel tank capacity	5 gallons
Cooling capacity	1.6 gallons
Crankcase oil capacity	3 quarts
Transmission and differential oil capacity	8 quarts
Tune-up	
Firing order	1-3-4-2
Spark plug used	Champion CJ-8
Spark plug gap	0.025 inches
Ignition point gap	0.022 inches
Timing	17 degrees BTDC (fan pulley)
Price	
Model G	$760 in 1949
Model G	$900 in 1951
Model G	$934 in 1953
Model G	$850 in 1955
Paint	

Tractor and wheels are Persian Orange. Hood transfers are black.

Options

Dual rear tires (each side)
1.6-mph slow gear
6-inch diameter by 4-inch wide belt pulley without hydraulics
Belt pulley (1,950 rpm) with a hydraulic lift assembly
Hand lift assembly
Air cleaner stack extension
Front end weight (141 pounds)
Master tool carrier

Comments

This small tractor was a product from the Allis Gadsden, Alabama, factory.

The rear engine design was advertised to give great visibility when working in crop rows and putting most of the tractor's weight over the rear wheels for greater traction.

Model G Standard Features

Adjustable wide front axle (36- to 64-inch tread)
Rear engine design with dual-tubular steel arched front frame
6-volt Delco-Remy 1109605 starter plus Guide brand lights
6.75-inch Bendix internal expanding rear foot-operated brakes

Rockford foot-operated clutch (6.5-inch plate)
Rochester gauges (oil pressure, water temperature, battery charge)

Production History (G models)

Year	Beginning number
1948	6
1949	10961
1950	23180
1951	24006
1952	25269
1953	26497
1954	28036
1955	29036
Ending serial number	29976

Allis-Chalmers Model WD
(total production approx. 146,525)

Nebraska test number	399 and 340
Serial numbers	7–146606
Location of serial number	at the left brake cover or left rear of axle housing
Location of engine number	left side of block, rear of carburetor
Production years	1948–1953
Total production	146,525 (approx.)
Engine	Allis-Chalmers vertical, four-cylinder I-head
Bore and stroke	4.0x4.0 inches
Rated rpm	1,400
Displacement	201 cubic inches
Compression ratio	
Gasoline	5.5:1
Tractor fuel	4.5:1
Fuel	gasoline or tractor fuel
Engine ratings (gasoline)	
Drawbar	30.23 horsepower
PTO/ belt	34.63 horsepower
Maximum pull	4,304 pounds
Speed	
First gear	2.5 mph
Second gear	3.5 mph
Third gear	4.75 mph
Fourth gear	9.0 mph
Reverse	2.0 mph
Length	128 inches
Rear tread	56–90 inches
Height (to top of steering wheel)	68 inches
Height (to top of muffler)	81.5 inches
Weight	3,388 pounds
Carburetor	Marvel-Schebler TSX-159 or Zenith 161AX

Ignition
   Prior to serial number 136318   Fairbanks-Morse magneto
   Serial number 136318 and up   Delco-Remy 1111745 distributor
Air cleaner   United (oil)
Front tire   5.5x16 inches
Rear tire   11x28 inches
Fuel tank capacity   15 gallons
Auxiliary fuel tank capacity
   (starting)   1 gallon
Cooling capacity   3.5 gallons
Crankcase oil capacity   6 quarts
Transmission and differential
   oil capacity   17 quarts
With PTO/belt pulley assembly   add 1 quart
Final drive oil capacity (each)   1 quart
Tune-up
   Firing order   1-2-4-3
   Spark plug used (gasoline)   Champion CJ-8
   Spark plug gap   0.035 inches
   Ignition point gap   0.020 inches
   Timing   30 degrees BTDC (flywheel)
Price
Model WD (narrow, dual front tires) $1,830 in 1953
Model WD (wide or single front tire) $1,960 in 1953
Paint
The tractor and wheels were painted Persian Orange and the rear rims are silver. Hood transfers are black. Starting in 1953, model designation transfers were used on the grille sides.

Options

12x28-inch rear tires
Adjustable wide front axle (adjustment ranges of 52 to 84 inches)
Single front eight-ply tire (9.00x10 inches)
9-inch diameter x 6.5-inch wide belt pulley assembly (1,260 rpm)
Front wheel weights (93 pounds each)
Rear wheel weights (142 pounds each)
Traction-Booster indicator
Seat cushion

Comments

The WD was an improved version of the older Model WC with more horsepower and many new features.

Engine numbers for the Model WD followed by the letter "K" will run on low octane fuels as well as gasoline. If a "G" follows the engine number, it was designed for gasoline exclusively.

Starting with 1952 serial number 127008 and up, the four-speed transmission was changed to a constant-mesh style to replace the previous sliding-gear style that had straight-cut teeth. The old style transmission had a straight gearshift lever unlike the curved shifter on the newer version.

At 1953 serial number 136318, the Fairbanks-Morse magneto was replaced by the Delco-Remy battery ignition system.

Field conversion kits were available to convert the tractor into different wheel configurations. Figures derived from Norm Swinford's book, *Allis-Chalmers Farm Equipment 1914–1985*, shows the Model WD being factory built in the following configurations and numbers:

Model WD (narrow, dual front)	112,358
Model WD (adjustable wide front)	29,846
Model WD (single front wheel)	1,074
Model WD (cotton picker)	2,419
Model WD (cane)	428

Model WD Standard Features
Narrow, dual wheel front axle (8-foot turning radius with brakes)
Power-Shift rear wheels (10 tread adjustments possible)
Traction-Booster system (hydraulic draft)
Double-acting shock-absorber seat
6-volt Delco-Remy 1107951 or Auto-Lite MCL6104 starter
Guide brand lights
Foot-operated rear brakes
PTO assembly (548 rpm)
Transmission hand-clutch (7-inch double plate in oil)

Production History (WD models)

Year	*Beginning number*
1948	7
1949	9250
1950	35445
1951	72328
1952	105182
1953	131243
Ending serial number	146606

Allis-Chalmers Model CA (total production 39,500)

Nebraska test number	453
Serial numbers	14–39513
Location of serial number	top of transmission by shifter
Location of engine number	left side of block on rear flange
Production years	1950–1958
Total production	39,500
Engine	Allis-Chalmers vertical, four-cylinder I-head
Bore and stroke	3.375x3.5 inches
Rated rpm	1,650
Displacement	125 cubic inches
Compression ratio	6.25:1
Fuel	gasoline
Engine ratings	
Drawbar	22.97 horsepower
PTO/ belt	25.96 horsepower

Maximum pull	3,557 pounds
Speed	
First gear	2.0 mph
Second gear	3.5 mph
Third gear	4.5 mph
Fourth gear	11.25 mph
Reverse	3.5 mph
Length	124.625 inches
Rear tread	52–80 inches
Height (to top of muffler)	76.275 inches
Weight	2,850 pounds
Carburetor	Zenith or Marvel-Schebler
Ignition	
Magneto	
(prior to engine no. CE149840)	Fairbanks-Morse FMJ or FMX4B3
Battery ignition	Delco-Remy 1111735
Air cleaner	Donaldson
Front tire	5.00x15 inches
Rear tire	10x24 inches
Fuel tank capacity	13 gallons
Auxiliary fuel tank capacity	
(starting)	1 gallon
Cooling capacity	2 gallons
Crankcase oil capacity	4 quarts
Transmission and differential	
oil capacity	8 quarts
With belt pulley/PTO assembly	add 1 quart
Final drive oil capacity (each)	0.75 quarts
Tune-up	
Firing order	1-2-4-3
Spark plug used	Champion CJ-8
Spark plug gap	0.032 inches
Ignition point gap	0.020 inches
Timing	30 degrees BTDC (flywheel)
Price	
Model CA (dual front, narrow axle)	$1,495 in 1954
Model CA (adjustable wide axle)	$1,540 in 1954
Model CA (single front wheel)	$1,540 in 1954
Paint	

Tractor and wheels are Persian Orange with silver-colored rear Power-Shift rims. "Allis-Chalmers" transfers on the hood sides are black. "CA" model designation is on the grille side with the bottom of transfer at the approximate grille mesh centerline.

Options

Axle clutch (right side, hand-operated)
Adjustable wide front axle
Single front wheel (6x12-inch tire)
Cane (high-clearance version)
Snap-Coupler and drawbar

Lift arm latches (for Snap-Coupler implements)
Rear wheel weights (145 pounds each)
Side weights (90 pounds each)
Seat cushion
Traction-Booster indicator
Rear wheel spacer set (88-inch maximum rear tread)
Remote ram
Single front wheel field conversion kit

Comments

A hand-operated clutch on the right axle shaft allowed the tractor to stop while the PTO and hydraulics still operated. This single plate, dry disc-type Lambert clutch was a very popular option that became a standard feature on later models.

According to figures derived from Norm Swinford's book, *Allis-Chalmers Farm Equipment 1914–1985*, the Model CA was made in the following configurations and numbers:

Model CA (narrow, dual front)	21,410 units built
Model CA (adjustable wide front)	17,439 units built
Model CA (single front wheel)	460 units built
Model CA (cane version)	190 units built

Model CA Standard Features

Narrow, dual front axle
Fenders
Power-Shift rear wheels
6-volt Delco-Remy 1107096 starter plus lights
4-speed constant-mesh transmission
Radiator shutters
PTO assembly (538 rpm)
Swinging drawbar (30-inch lateral adjustment)
Hydraulic control system (3,500-pound relief piston pump)
8-inch diameter by 5.5-inch wide belt pulley

Production History (CA models)

Year	Beginning number
1950	14
1951	322
1952	10539
1953	22181
1954	31424
1955	32907
1956	37203
1957	38618
1958	38977
Ending serial number	39513

Allis-Chalmers Model WD-45 (total production 90,352)

Nebraska test numbers	499/511/512/563
Serial numbers	146607–236958
Location of serial number	
Gasoline, distillate, and propane	on rear face of transmission
Diesel	at left brake cover or transmission housing (left rear)
Location of engine number	left side of block
Production years	1953–1957
Total production	
(all WD-45 models)	90,352
Engine	
Gasoline, distillate, and LPG	Allis-Chalmers vertical, four-cylinder I-head
Diesel	Allis-Chalmers vertical, 6-cylinder injected
Bore and stroke	
Gasoline, distillate, and LPG	4x4.5 inches
Diesel	3.4375x4.125 inches
Rated rpm	
Gasoline, distillate, and LPG	1,400
Diesel	1,625
Displacement	
Gasoline, distillate, and LPG	226 cubic inches
Diesel	230 cubic inches
Compression ratio	
Gasoline	6.45:1
Distillate	4.75:1
LPG	7.2:1
Diesel	15.5:1
Engine ratings	
Gasoline (test no. 499)	
Drawbar	37.84 horsepower
PTO/belt	43.21 horsepower
Maximum pull	5,441 pounds
Distillate (test no. 511)	
Drawbar	29.49 horsepower
PTO/belt	33.01 horsepower
Maximum pull	4,634 pounds
LPG (test no. 512)	
Drawbar	38.53 horsepower
PTO/belt	44.13 horsepower
Maximum pull	5,421 pounds
Diesel (test no. 563)	
Drawbar	39.50 horsepower
PTO/belt	43.29 horsepower
Maximum pull	5,908 pounds
Speed (all WD-45 models)	
First gear	2.4 mph
Second gear	3.75 mph
Third gear	5.0 mph
Fourth gear	11.25 mph
Reverse	3.25 mph

Length
  Gasoline, distillate, and LPG   127.1 inches
  Diesel   128 inches
Rear tread   56–90 inches
Height (to top of muffler)
  Gasoline, distillate, and LPG   81.5 inches
  Diesel models   88.25 inches
Weight (shipping)
  Gasoline   4,465 pounds
  Distillate   4,465 pounds
  LPG   4,640 pounds
  Diesel   4,730 pounds
Carburetor
  Gasoline   Marvel-Schebler TSX464
  Distillate   Marvel-Schebler TSX561
  LPG   Ensign Kg1 or Kgn1
Injector pump (diesel)   Bosch PSB
Ignition (non-diesel models)   Delco-Remy 1111745
Air cleaner   United (oil)
Front tire   5.5x16 inches
Rear tire   12x28 inches
Fuel tank capacity (not LPG)   15 gallons
Cooling capacity
  Gasoline, distillate, and LPG   3.5 gallons
  Diesel   4.25 gallons
Crankcase oil capacity
  Gasoline, distillate, and LPG   6 quarts
  Diesel   7 quarts
Transmission oil capacity   17 quarts
Final drive oil capacity (each)   1.75 quarts
Tune-up
  Firing order
    Gasoline, distillate, and LPG   1-2-4-3
    Diesel   1-5-3-6-2-4
  Spark plug used
    Gasoline   Champion J-12YC
    Distillate   Champion J-14Y
  Spark plug gap   0.030 inches
  Ignition point gap   0.020 inches
  Timing
    Gasoline, distillate, and LPG   30 degrees BTDC (flywheel)
    Diesel   21 degrees BTDC (flywheel)
Prices (1955 with dual, narrow front axle)
  Gasoline $2,155
  LPG $2,410
  Diesel $3,005
Paint
Tractor and wheels are Persian Orange with silver Power-Shift rims.

Options
Adjustable wide front axle (52–84-inch tread)
9.00x10-inch single front wheel

Cane (high-clearance version)
11x28-inch rear tires
LPG conversion equipment
Snap-Coupler and drawbar for Snap-Coupler models
Lift arm latches for Snap-Coupler models
9-inch diameter by 6.5-inch wide belt pulley
  (Belt pulley speeds of 1,260 rpm/gas and 1,462 rpm/diesel)
Remote ram
Front inner wheel weights (93 pounds each)
Front outer wheel weights (157 pounds each)
Rear wheel weights (142 pounds each)
Seat cushion
Traction-Booster indicator
Power steering (introduced in 1956)

Comments

The WD-45 was a direct descendant of the WD and WC models. More power plus the Traction-Booster draft system gave this newer model a huge advantage over the WD and WC models.

According to the production figures derived from Norm Swinford's book, *Allis-Chalmers Farm Equipment 1914–1985*, the WD-45 tractor was made in the following configurations and numbers:

Model WD-45 gas (adjustable wide front)	45,730 units built
Model WD-45 gas (narrow, dual front)	36,896 units built
Model WD-45 gas (single front wheel)	824 units built
Model WD-45 gas (cane version)	86 units built
Model WD-45 diesel (adj. wide front)	5,165 units built
Model WD-45 diesel (narrow, dual front)	1,240 units built
Model WD-45 diesel (single front wheel)	47 units built
Model WD-45 diesel (cane version)	57 units built

Model WD-45 Gasoline, Distillate, and LPG Standard Features
Dual narrow front axle
Power-Crater engine
Snap-Coupler hitch (standard feature at serial no. 151381 and up)
Traction-Booster draft system (3,500-pound relief piston pump)
Power-Shift rear wheels
Drawbar (5-inch lateral adjustment)
PTO assembly (548 rpm)
Rockford 10-inch dry master clutch plus wet clutch for the PTO
6-volt Delco-Remy 1107951 starter and Guide brand lights

Model WD-45 Diesel Standard Features
Production commenced in October 1954 with serial no. 181341
Traction-Booster draft system
Two-clutch power control
Power-Shift rear wheels
Drawbar (5-inch lateral adjustment)
PTO assembly (548 rpm)
12-volt Delco-Remy 1113035 or 1108998 starter
Guide brand lights

Production History (all WD-45 models)

Year	Beginning number
1953	146607
1954	160386
1955	190993
1956	217992
1957	230295
Ending serial number	236958

Allis-Chalmers Model D-14 (total production 22,286)

Nebraska test numbers	623 and 645
Serial numbers	1001–24050
Location of serial number	left, front side of torque housing
Location of engine number	left side of block rear of carburetor
Production years	1957–1960
Total production	22,286
Engine	Allis-Chalmers vertical, four-cylinder I-head
Bore and stroke	3.50x3.875 inches
Rated rpm	1,650
Displacement	149 cubic inches
Compression ratio	
Gasoline	7.5:1
LPG	8.5:1
Fuel	gasoline, distillate, or LPG
Engine ratings	
Gasoline (test 623)	
Drawbar	30.91 horsepower
PTO/ belt	34.08 horsepower
Maximum pull	4,847 pounds
LPG (test 645)	
Drawbar	28.67 horsepower
PTO/belt	31.86 horsepower
Maximum pull	5,023 pounds
Speed	
D-14 Standard or Grove models	
High-range	
First gear	2.2 mph
Second gear	3.75 mph
Third gear	4.75 mph
Fourth gear	12.0 mph
Reverse	3.75 mph
Low-range (Power-Director)	
First gear	1.5 mph
Second gear	2.6 mph
Third gear	3.4 mph
Fourth gear	8.5 mph
Reverse	2.6 mph
D-14 High-Clearance	
High-range	
First gear	2.6 mph

Second gear	4.6 mph
Third gear	5.9 mph
Fourth gear	14.7 mph
Reverse	4.6 mph
Low-range (Power-Director)	
First gear	1.8 mph
Second gear	3.2 mph
Third gear	4.1 mph
Fourth gear	10.4 mph
Reverse	3.2 mph
Length	129 inches
Rear tread	54 to 80 inches
Height (to top of muffler)	79.56 inches
Height (to top of hood)	55.875 inches
Weight	4,200 pounds
Carburetor	
Gasoline and distillate	Marvel-Schebler TSX-670 or TSX-701
LPG	Ensign MG 1
Ignition (prior to serial number 19001)	Delco-Remy 1111745
Ignition (serial number 19001 and after)	Delco-Remy 1112593
Air cleaner	Donaldson
Front tire	5.50x16 inches
Rear tire	11x26 inches
Fuel tank capacity (gasoline)	14.5 gallons
Auxiliary fuel tank capacity (starting)	0.75 gallons
LPG tank capacity (80 percent usable volume)	15.8 gallons
Cooling capacity	9 quarts
Crankcase oil capacity	4 quarts
Transmission oil capacity	14.5 quarts
Final drive oil capacity (each)	0.625 quarts
Power-Director clutch oil capacity	10 quarts
Tune-up	
Firing order	1-2-4-3
Spark plug used	
Gasoline	Champion J-11
LPG	Champion J-3
Spark plug gap	0.030 inches
Ignition point gap	0.020 inches
Timing (full advance using timing light)	marked "Fire" on flywheel
Price (gasoline, tricycle)	
Model D-14 (gasoline, narrow front)	$2,875 in 1960
Model D-14 (High-Clearance)	$3,275 in 1960
Model D-14 (Orchard)	$3,770 in 1960
Model D-14 (LPG option)	add $310 in 1960

Paint

Prior to serial number 18230, the tractor is painted Persian Orange with orange wheels and grille, plus silver rear rims. The hood transfers are silver.

Beginning in 1959 at serial number 19001, the all-orange grille was changed to silver with black horizontal bars and border, and the hood transfers are white with black letters. The black-bar grille appeared on 5,050 units.

Industrial versions were often painted yellow.

Options

Roll-Shift adjustable wide front axle

Single front wheel (9.00x10-inch)

12x26-inch rear tires

Orchard conversion kit

High-clearance model

Snap-Coupler adapter to three-point hitch

Power-Director release (throws into neutral if draft obstructed)

Power steering

Transport valve (hydraulic outlet)

Horn

Low-clearance muffler

Operation meter (rpm and hours)

Removable rear warning light (with outlet plug)

Rear wheel weights (quarter sections, 65 pounds each)

Front wheel weights (90 pounds each)

9-inch diameter by 6.5-inch wide shiftable belt pulley (1,384 rpm)

Shuttle clutch (reverses direction of tractor in any gear)

Comments

In 1959, a silver grille with three black horizontal bands and border was used for aesthetics. It started with serial number 19001.

Engine numbers followed by "S" or no letter are designed for low-octane fuel. Engine numbers followed by "M" are designed for gasoline.

The Grove models were usually dealer conversions of standard models, and the numbers produced are uncertain.

Production figures derived from Norm Swinford's *Allis-Chalmers Farm Equipment 1914–1985* shows the D-14 was built in the following configurations and numbers:

Model D-14 (narrow, dual front)	4,662 units built
Model D-14 (Roll-Shift wide front)	17,564 units built
Model D-14 (single front wheel)	54 units built
Model D-14 (High-Clearance)	6 units built
Model D-14 (LPG fuel)	approx. 750 units built

Other dealer-supplied field conversion kits for grove, high-clearance, LPG, and different front axle styles may change the actual totals from the factory built totals.

Model D-14 Standard Features

Dual, narrow front axle (97-inch turning radius)

Power-Director (two-range speed control)

6-volt Delco-Remy 1107474 starter plus lights

PTO assembly (549 rpm)

Power-Shift rear wheels (2.5-inch increments)

Model D-14 High-Clearance Standard Features
10x38- or 11.2x38-inch rear tires
Approx. 4.5 inches higher than standard model (10x38-inch tires)
28.5-inch clearance (tricycle)
Power-Director (two-range speed control)
6-volt Delco-Remy 1107474 starter plus lights
PTO assembly (549 rpm)

Model D-14 Grove Standard Features
Adjustable wide front axle with undermounted headlights
26-inch rear turf tires
Rear citrus fenders and operator screen guard
Grille screen guard
6-volt Delco-Remy 1107474 starter
Power-Director (two-range speed control)
PTO assembly (549 rpm)

Model D-14 Industrial Standard Features
Fixed-tread, heavy-duty wide front axle
12.4x26-inch four-ply industrial rear tires
Shuttle clutch (reverses direction of all gears)
Power steering
Heavy-duty clutch
6-volt Delco-Remy starter plus lights

Production History (all D-14 models)

Year	Beginning number
1957	1001
1958	9400
1959	14900
1960	21800
Ending serial number	24050

Allis-Chalmers Model D-17 (total production approximately 62,867)

Nebraska test numbers	635/636/644
Serial numbers	1001–89213
Location of serial number	left, front side of torque housing
Location of engine number	left side of block rear of carburetor
Production years	1957–1967
Total production	62,867 approx.
Engine	
Nondiesel models	Allis-Chalmers vertical, four-cylinder I-head
Diesel	Allis Chalmers vertical, six-cylinder I-head
Bore and stroke	
Nondiesel models	4.0x4.5 inches

Diesel	3.563x4.375 inches
Rated rpm (all models)	1,650
Displacement	
Nondiesel models	226 cubic inches
Diesel	262 cubic inches
Compression ratio	
Gasoline	7.5:1
LPG	8.25:1
Diesel	15.7:1
Engine ratings	
Gasoline (test no. 635)	
Drawbar	48.64 horsepower
PTO/belt	52.70 horsepower
Maximum pull	7,059 pounds
LPG (test no. 644)	
Drawbar	46.23 horsepower
PTO/belt	50.79 horsepower
Maximum pull	6,956 pounds
Diesel (test no. 636)	
Drawbar	46.20 horsepower
PTO/belt	51.14 horsepower
Maximum pull	7,156 pounds
Speed (all D-17 models except High-Clearance)	
High-range	
First gear	2.6 mph
Second gear	4.0 mph
Third gear	5.4 mph
Fourth gear	11.9 mph
Reverse	3.4 mph
Low-range (Power-Director)	
First gear	1.8 mph
Second gear	2.9 mph
Third gear	3.8 mph
Fourth gear	8.3 mph
Reverse	2.4 mph
Speed (D-17 High-Clearance models)	
High-range	
First gear	2.9 mph
Second gear	4.6 mph
Third gear	6.2 mph
Fourth gear	13.6 mph
Reverse	3.9 mph
Low-range (Power-Director)	
First gear	2.1 mph
Second gear	3.3 mph
Third gear	4.4 mph
Fourth gear	9.5 mph
Reverse	2.8 mph
Length	140 inches
Rear tread	58–92 inches
Height (to top of muffler)	81 inches

Height (to top of hood)	60.625 inches
Weight (shipping)	
Gasoline	5,300 pounds
LPG	5,500 pounds
Diesel	5,500 pounds
High-Clearance	additional 80 pounds
Carburetor	
Gasoline	Zenith 267J8 or Marvel-Schebler TSX-464, TSX-561, TSX-773, or TSX-871
LPG	Ensign Mg 1
Diesel injector pump	Roosa-Master
Ignition (prior to engine number 17-19978)	Delco-Remy 1112584
Ignition (engine number 17-19978 and up)	Delco-Remy 1112593
Air cleaner	dry element
Front tire	6.00x16 inches
Rear tire	
Prior to serial number 42001	13x28 inches
Serial number 42001 and up	14.9x28 inches
Fuel tank capacity (non-LPG models)	20.8 gallons
Auxiliary fuel tank (starting)	0.75 gallons
LPG tank capacity (80 percent usable volume)	22.3 gallons
Cooling capacity	14.5 quarts
Crankcase oil capacity (all versions)	6 quarts
Transmission oil capacity	7 gallons
Power-Director oil capacity	2.5 gallons
Final drive oil capacity (each)	1.25 quarts
Tune-up	
Firing order	
Gasoline and LPG	1-2-4-3
Diesel	1-5-3-6-2-4
Spark plug used	
Gasoline (prior to engine no. 17293)	Champion J8-C
Gasoline (engine no. 17293 and after)	Champion N-8
LPG (all)	Champion N-3
Spark plug gap	
Gasoline	0.025 inches
LPG	0.020 inches
Ignition point gap	0.022 inches
Timing	

(advanced, timing light, for nondiesel at flywheel timing hole)
   D-17 engine numbers prior to 17-19978 "F" at top hole
   D-17 engine number 17-19978 and up   "F" in center of hole
   (Timing for diesel, see tune-up for D-15 Series I)

Model D-17

Price

Model D-17 (gasoline, tricycle)	$4,053 in 1962
Model D-17 (gasoline, High-Clearance)	$4,197 in 1962
Model D-17 (gasoline, Orchard)	$4,610 in 1962
Model D-17 (gasoline, Grove)	$4,393 in 1962
Model D-17 (gasoline, Wheatland)	$4,473 in 1962
Model D-17 (gasoline, Rice)	$4,574 in 1962
Model D-17 (diesel option)	add $895 in 1962
Model D-17 (LPG option)	add $319.50 in 1962

Paint

Serial numbers 1001 to 23363 have the tractor, grille, and wheels painted Persian Orange with silver wheel rims and hood transfers.

Serial numbers 24001 to 31625 are the same as the previous models with the difference of three black horizontal bars and border on a silver radiator grille plus white and black hood transfers.

Serial numbers 32001 to 41540, referred to as the Series II, have the tractor painted Persian Orange no. 2 (a redder color) and the wheels and grille (no bars) painted a cream color. The cylinder-shaped muffler and wheel rims are silver. The hood has cream-colored metal hood plaques.

Series III, serial numbers 42001 to 72768, have the same colors as the Series II with the changes being a large, black oval muffler and large cream-colored hood transfers.

Serial numbers 75001 until the end of production are Series IV and are the same colors as Series III, but have the series designation on the fuel tank decal.

The industrial version is usually painted light yellow.

Options

Heavy-duty adjustable or nonadjustable wide front axle
Power steering
Dual, narrow front axle
6.5x16-inch single front wheel (9.00x10-inch for High-Clearance)
Front wheel weights (90 pounds each)
Rear wheel weights (quarter sections, 75 pounds each)
Orchard conversion kit
Snap-Coupler adapter to three-point hitch
Power-Director release (throws into neutral if draft obstructed)
9-inch diameter by 6.56-inch wide belt pulley (1,384 rpm)
Taillight
Operation meter (rpm and hours)
Foot accelerator (utility industrial)

Comments

Engine numbers followed by "S" are designed for low-octane fuels. Engine numbers followed by "M" are designed for gasoline.

D-17 models prior to serial 32001 are unofficially called Series I. (There were 29,988 built.)

Series II started at 1960 serial number 32001 (9,540 were built).

Series III started at 1962 serial number 42001 (9,126 were built).

Series IV started at 1964 serial number 75001 (14,213 were built).

Series IV models (serial numbers 75001 and later) have live hydraulics and a category 2 three-point hitch option.

Series III and IV D-17 models have band/disc brakes to replace the external drum brakes on previous models.

Some 1,815 LPG versions were built from 1958 to 1962 (other years are unknown).

Model D-17 Standard Features

Power-Director (two-range speed control)
Adjustable wide front axle
Power-Shift rear wheels
Traction-Booster draft system
Live 549-rpm PTO and hydraulics (Series IV)
6-volt Delco-Remy 1107466 starter (early gasoline models)
12-volt Delco-Remy 1107695 starter (later gasoline models)
12-volt Delco-Remy 11133082 or 1113152 starter (diesel models)

Model D-17 Orchard Standard Features

Power-Director (two-range speed control)
Grille and operator guard plus full citrus fenders
Downward exhaust
Roll-Shift front axle with undermounted lights
Standard rear rims with 16.9x26-inch tires

Model D-17 Grove Standard Features

Power-Director (two-range speed control)
Roll-Shift front axle
18.4x26-inch six-ply rear tires

Model D-17 Wheatland Standard Features

Power-Director (two-range speed control)
Full-width fenders
Heavy-duty swinging drawbar
18.4x28-inch rear tires on standard rear rims

Model D-17 Rice Standard Features

Power-Director (two-range speed control)
Heavy-duty swinging drawbar
13x28-, 15x28-, or 18.4x28-inch rice tires
Standard rear rims
Mud shields

Model D-17 Industrial Standard Features

Heavy-duty, fixed-tread wide front axle
14.9x28-inch, six-ply industrial rear tires
Power steering and live PTO
Heavy-duty clutch
Heavy-duty swinging drawbar
Heavy-duty rear wheels
Shuttle clutch (reverses all gears)

Model D-17 High-Clearance Standard Features
Available in single front wheel or special Roll-Shift front axle
16.5x16-inch (single) or 7.50x20-inch (Roll-Shift) front tires
13.6x38-inch rear cane tires
Power-Director (two-range speed control)
Long-drop final drive housings and front spindles
85-inch height
26-inch crop clearance (adjustable wide front axle)
Rear tread of 60 to 96 inches
Shipping weight of 5,760 pounds (nondiesel)
Shipping weight of 6,025 pounds (diesel)

Production History (all D-17 models)

Year	Beginning number
1957	1001
1958	4300
1959	16500
1960	28200
1961	33100
1962	38070
1963	65001
1964	70611
1965	77090
1966	80533
1967	86061
Ending serial number	89213

Allis-Chalmers offered the popular D-17 in diesel and liquid propane gas versions as well as the popular gasoline version. More than 12,000 units were built in 1958 alone.

The D-10 was the proud offspring of the one-row Model B. The similar Model D-12 had a wider wheel spacing to straddle two crop rows. Although these models were well-built machines, sales were only moderate as the average farmer was looking for a larger tractor. A real delight to a tractor collector is to acquire a D-10 with the three black bars across the radiator. The exact numbers are not known, but less than 950 units were built this way until 1960. The later D-10 models had no black bars and were painted the newer Persian Orange no. 2.

Allis-Chalmers Model D-10, G138 Engine (total production approximately 2,148)

Nebraska test number	724
Serial numbers (all D-10 models)	1001–10100
Serial numbers (G138 engine models)	1001–3262
Location of serial number	left, front side of torque housing
Location of engine number	left side of block rear of carburetor
Production years (all D-10 models)	1959–1968
Production years (G138 engine models)	1959–1961
Total production (all D-10 models)	5,308 (approx.)
Total production (G138 engine models)	2,148 (approx.)
Engine	Allis-Chalmers vertical, four-cylinder I-head
Bore and stroke	3.375x3.875 inches
Rated rpm	1,650
Displacement	138.7 cubic inches
Compression ratio	7.75:1
Fuel	gasoline

Engine ratings

Drawbar	25.73 horsepower
PTO/belt	28.51 horsepower
Maximum pull	3,555 pounds

Speed
  D-10

First gear	1.9 mph
Second gear	3.3 mph
Third gear	4.3 mph
Fourth gear	11.5 mph
Reverse	3.3 mph

  D-10 High-Clearance

First gear	2.5 mph
Second gear	4.4 mph
Third gear	5.6 mph
Fourth gear	14.2 mph
Reverse	4.4 mph

Length	121 inches
Rear tread	42–72 inches
Height (overall)	76.5 inches
Weight	2,860 pounds
Carburetor	Zenith 161J7
Ignition	Delco-Remy 1112593
Air cleaner	Donaldson
Front tire	4.00x15 inches
Rear tire	10x24 inches
Fuel tank capacity	12 gallons
Cooling capacity	2 gallons
Crankcase oil capacity	4.5 quarts
Transmission/differential oil capacity	6.5 quarts
With PTO/belt pulley and plunger pump	add 2.25 quarts
Final drive oil capacity (each)	1 quart

Tune-up

Firing order	1-2-4-3
Spark plug used	Champion J-11
Spark plug gap	0.025 inches
Ignition point gap	0.022 inches
Timing	25 degrees BTDC (flywheel)

Price	$1,810 in 1960

Paint

D-10 tractors prior to serial number 1950 are painted Persian Orange and the grilles are silver with a black border and three black horizontal bars. The wheels are orange with silver rims.

Serial numbers after 1950 and before 3501 are Persian Orange no. 2 and have plain cream-colored grilles and bars plus cream wheels with silver rims.

The industrial version is usually painted yellow.

Options

Power-Shift rear wheel rims

9x24-inch rear tires or 5.00x15-inch front tires

8-inch diameter x 5.5-inch wide belt pulley (1,220 rpm)

Rear wheel weights (106 pounds each)
Power steering
Operation meter (rpm and hours)

Comments

All Model D-10 tractors made until serial number 6801 are referred to as Series I models (3,172 units). All D-10 tractors made at serial number 3501 and after have a larger 149-cubic inch displacement with the bore increased from 3.375 inches to 3.5 inches. There are three series of the D-10 tractor.

A high-clearance version and an industrial model with a heavier front axle were available.

Model D-10 (G138 engine) Standard Features
Reversible-dish rear wheels with four-position rims
6-volt Delco-Remy 1107474 starter with lights
Adjustable wide front axle (40- to 64-inch tread width)
7-inch brake drums with internal expanding shoes
PTO assembly (538 rpm)
20.25-inch crop clearance
Ammeter, oil, and fuel gauges

Model D-10 High-Clearance (G138 engine) Standard Features
9x36-inch rear tires (11.2x36 optional)
5.5x16-inch front tires
81-inch overall height and 24.5-inch crop clearance
43- to 71-inch adjustable tread
Adjustable wide front axle
Shipping weight of 3,240 pounds

Model D-10 Industrial (G138 engine) Standard Features
11.2x24-inch industrial four-ply rear tires
6.00x16-inch six-ply front tires
Heavy-duty clutch
Heavy-duty, nonadjustable wide front axle
Power steering (hydrostatic)

Production History (all D-10 models)

Year	Beginning number
1959	1001
1960	1950
1961	2801
1962	4522
1963	6801
1964	7675
1965	9204
1966	9486
1967	9795
1968	9979
Ending serial number	10100

Allis-Chalmers Model D-10, G149 Engine (total production approximately 3,160)

Nebraska test number	812
Serial numbers (all D-10 models)	1001–10100
Serial numbers (G149 engine models)	3501–10100
Location of serial numbers	left, front side of torque housing
Location of engine number	left side of block rear of carburetor
Production years (all D-10 models)	1959–1968
Production years (G149 engine models)	1961–1968
Total production (all D-10 models)	5,308 (approx.)
Total production (G149 engine models)	3,160 (approx.)
Engine	Allis-Chalmers vertical, four-cylinder I-head
Bore and stroke	3.50x3.875 inches
Rated rpm	1,650
Displacement	149 cubic inches
Compression ratio	7.5:1
Fuel	gasoline
Engine ratings	
Drawbar	28.78 horsepower
PTO/belt	33.46 horsepower
Maximum pull	4,106 pounds
Speed	
D-10	
First gear	2.0 mph
Second gear	3.5 mph
Third gear	4.5 mph
Fourth gear	11.4 mph
Reverse	3.5 mph
D-10 High-Clearance	
First gear	2.5 mph
Second gear	4.4 mph
Third gear	5.6 mph
Fourth gear	14.2 mph
Reverse	4.4 mph
Length	121 inches
Rear tread	42–72 inches
Height (overall)	76.5 inches
Weight	3,001 pounds
Carburetor	Zenith 161J7
Ignition	Delco-Remy 1112609
Air cleaner	Donaldson
Front tire	5.00x15 inches
Rear tire	11x24 inches
Fuel tank capacity	12 gallons
Cooling capacity	2 gallons
Crankcase oil capacity	4.5 quarts
Transmission oil capacity	6.5 quarts
With two-range speed option	add 6 quarts
With PTO and hydraulic pump	add 5 quarts

87

Final drive oil capacity (each)	1 quart
Tune-up	
Firing order	1-2-4-3
Spark plug used	Champion J-11
Spark plug gap	0.025 inches
Ignition point gap	0.022 inches
Timing	25 degrees BTDC (flywheel)
Price	
Model D-10 (standard)	$2,659 in 1962
Model D-10 (standard)	$3,420 in 1968
Paint	

All D-10 farm models with the 149-cubic inch engine are painted Persian Orange no. 2 and have cream-colored grilles and wheels with silver rear rims. The industrial D-10 models are normally painted yellow.

Options

Deluxe seat
Power-Shift rear wheel rims
9x24-inch rear tires or 5.00x15-inch front tires
8-inch diameter x 5.5-inch wide belt pulley (1,220 rpm)
Rear wheel weights (106 pounds each)
Dual rear wheels
Two-range transmission (Series III)
Operation meter (rpm and hours)

Comments

Serial numbers after 6801 and before 9001 are referred to as Series II (approximately 1,050 units) and had no significant changes from the later Series I models that had the G149 engine.

D-10 tractors at serial number 9001 and up are referred to as Series III (approximately 1,084 units) and had lights mounted on the rear fenders and a black oval muffler to replace the earlier cylinder-shaped muffler that was painted silver.

Series III models offered an optional two-range transmission and an optional hydraulic midmount lift.

A high-clearance version was available as well as an industrial model with a heavier front axle. Starting in 1964, the D-10 Series II industrial version was replaced by the I-40. The I-40 was painted yellow and had a heavy-duty, box-shaped grille, but otherwise was pretty much the same tractor. The I-400 replaced the almost identical I-40 in 1966.

Model D-10 (G149 engine) Standard Features

Reversible-dish rear wheels with four-position rims
12-volt Delco-Remy 1107265 starter with lights
Adjustable wide front axle (40- to 64-inch tread)
Traction-Booster draft system
Live PTO assembly (538 rpm)

Model D-10 High-Clearance (G149 engine) Standard Features

9x36-inch rear tires (11.2x36 optional)
5.5x16-inch front tires
81-inch overall height and 24.5-inch crop clearance
43- to 71-inch adjustable rear tread

Model D-10 Series II Industrial (G149 engine) Standard Features

11.2x24-inch industrial four-ply rear tires
6.00x16-inch six-ply front tires
Heavy-duty, nonadjustable wide front axle
Heavy-duty clutch
Three-point hitch (draft responsive)
Power steering (hydrostatic)
Padded seat

Allis-Chalmers Model D-12, G138 Engine (total production approximately 1,747)

Nebraska test number	723
Serial numbers (all D-12 models)	1001–10172
Serial numbers (G138 engine models)	1001–2919
Location of serial number	left, front side of torque housing
Location of engine number	left side of block rear of carburetor
Production years (all D-12 models)	1959–1968
Production years (G138 engine models)	1959–1961
Total production (all D-12 models)	4,201 (approx.)
Total production (G138 engine models)	1,747 (approx.)
Engine	Allis-Chalmers vertical, four-cylinder I-head
Bore and stroke	3.375x3.875 inches
Rated rpm	1,650
Displacement	138.7 cubic inches
Compression ratio	7.75:1
Fuel	gasoline
Engine ratings	
Drawbar	23.56 horsepower
PTO/belt	28.56 horsepower
Maximum pull	4,041 pounds
Speed	
D-12	
First gear	2.0 mph
Second gear	3.5 mph
Third gear	4.5 mph
Fourth gear	11.4 mph
Reverse	3.5 mph
D-12 High-Clearance	
First gear	2.5 mph
Second gear	4.4 mph
Third gear	5.6 mph
Fourth gear	14.2 mph
Reverse	4.4 mph

Length	121 inches
Rear tread	52–79 inches
Height (to top of hood)	52.5 inches
Weight	2,945 pounds
Carburetor	Zenith 161J7
Ignition	Delco-Remy 1112593
Air cleaner	Donaldson
Front tire	5.00x15 inches
Rear tire	11x24 inches
Fuel tank capacity	12 gallons
Cooling capacity	2 gallons
Crankcase oil capacity	4.5 quarts
Transmission/differential oil capacity	6.5 quarts
With PTO/belt pulley and plunger pump	add 2.25 quarts
Final drive oil capacity (each)	1 quart
Tune-up	
Firing order	1-2-4-3
Spark plug used	Champion J-11
Spark plug gap	0.025 inches
Ignition point gap	0.022 inches
Timing	25 degrees BTDC (flywheel)
Price	$2,766 in 1962
Paint	

D-12 tractors prior to serial number 1950 are painted Persian Orange and have grilles that are silver with a black border and three black horizontal bars. The wheels are orange with silver rims.

Serial numbers after 1950 and before number 3001 are Persian Orange no. 2 with a plain cream-colored grille and bars plus cream wheels with silver rims. Industrial models are usually painted yellow.

Options

8-inch diameter x 5.5-inch wide belt pulley (1,220 rpm)
Rear wheel weights (135 pounds each)
Operation meter (rpm and hours)

Comments

All D-12 models made before 1963 serial number 5501 are referred to as Series I (approximately 2,385 units). All models made before 1961 serial number 3001 have the G138 engine and all afterwards have the G149 engine. There are three series of the D-12 tractor.

Model D-12 (G138 engine) Standard Features

Power-Shift rear wheel rims with reversible-dish wheels
6-volt Delco-Remy 1107474 starter plus lights
Adjustable wide front axle (48- to 72-inch tread)
7-inch brake drums with internal expanding shoes
PTO assembly (538 rpm)
20.25-inch crop clearance
Ammeter, oil, and fuel gauges

Model D-12 High-Clearance (G138 engine) Standard Features
9x36- or 9.5x36-inch rear tires (11.2x36 optional)
5.5x16-inch front tires
6-volt Delco-Remy 1107474 starter plus lights
Adjustable wide front axle
81-inch overall height and 24.5-inch crop clearance
Adjustable tread of 52 to 80 inches
Shipping weight of 3,220 pounds

Model D-12 Industrial (G138 engine) Standard Features
11.2x24-inch rear tires and 6.00x16-inch front tires
6-volt Delco-Remy 1107474 starter plus lights
Heavy-duty nonadjustable wide front axle
Heavy-duty clutch
Three-point hitch (not draft responsive)

Production History (all D-12 models)

Year	Beginning number
1959	1001
1960	1950
1961	2801
1962	3638
1963	5501
1964	6012
1965	9192
1966	9508
1967	9830
1968	9979
Ending serial number	10172

Allis-Chalmers Model D-12, G149 Engine (total production approximately 2,454)

Nebraska test number	813
Serial numbers (all D-12 models)	1001–10172
Serial numbers (G149 engine models)	3001–10172
Location of serial number	left, front side of torque housing
Location of engine number	left side of block rear of carburetor
Production years (all D-12 models)	1959–1968
Production years (G149 engine models)	1961–1968
Total production (all D-12 models)	4,201(approx.)
Total production (G149 engine models)	2,454 (approx.)
Engine	Allis-Chalmers vertical, four-cylinder I-head
Bore and stroke	3.50x3.875 inches
Rated rpm	1,650

Displacement	149 cubic inches
Compression ratio	7.5:1
Fuel	gasoline
Engine ratings	
Drawbar	29.43 horsepower
PTO/belt	33.32 horsepower
Maximum pull	4,241 pounds
Speed	
D-12	
First gear	2.0 mph
Second gear	3.5 mph
Third gear	4.5 mph
Fourth gear	11.4 mph
Reverse	3.5 mph
D-12 High-Clearance	
First gear	2.5 mph
Second gear	4.4 mph
Third gear	5.6 mph
Fourth gear	14.2 mph
Reverse	4.4 mph
Length	121 inches
Rear tread	52–79 inches
Height (to top of hood)	52.5 inches
Weight	3,051 pounds
Carburetor	Zenith 161J7
Ignition	Delco-Remy 1112593
Air cleaner	Donaldson
Front tire	5.00x15 inches
Rear tire	11x24 inches
Fuel tank capacity	12 gallons
Cooling capacity	2 gallons
Crankcase oil capacity	4.5 quarts
Transmission/differential oil capacity	6.5 quarts
With two-range speed option	add 6 quarts
With PTO and hydraulic pump	add 5 quarts
Final drive oil capacity (each)	1 quart
Tune-up	
Firing order	1-2-4-3
Spark plug used	Champion J8-C
Spark plug gap	0.025 inches
Ignition point gap	0.022 inches
Timing	25 degrees BTDC (flywheel)
Price	
Model D-12 Series III (Traction-Booster)	$3,285 in 1967
Model D-12 Series III High-Clearance	$3,228 in 1967

Paint
All D-12 farm models with the G149 engine are painted Persian Orange no. 2 with cream-colored grilles and wheels. Rims are silver. Industrial models are usually painted yellow.

Options
Deluxe seat
8-inch diameter x 5.5-inch wide belt pulley (1,220 rpm)
Rear wheel weights (135 pounds each)
Three-point hitch
Two-range transmission (Series III)
Operation meter (rpm and hours)

Comments
Serial numbers after 1001 and before 5501 are referred to as Series I Models (approximately 2,385 units).
Serial numbers starting with 5501 and before 9001 are called Series II (approximately 644 units).
Serial numbers 9001 and after are called Series III (approximately 1,172 units).
Series III models had the headlights mounted on the fenders and had a black, oval muffler to replace the earlier cylindrical, silver type.
This series also offered an optional midmount hydraulic lift and an optional two-range transmission.
A high-clearance version and an industrial model with a heavier front axle were available. The Model I-40 replaced the D-12 Series II Industrial in 1964. The almost identical Model I-400 replaced the I-40 in 1966.

Model D-12 (G149 engine) Standard Features
Power-Shift rear wheel rims with reversible-dish wheels
12-volt Delco-Remy 1107265 starter with lights
Adjustable wide front axle
Live PTO assembly (538 rpm)
20.25-inch crop clearance
Ammeter, oil, and fuel gauges

Model D-12 High-Clearance (G149 engine) Standard Features
9x36-inch rear tires (11.2x36 optional)
5.50x16-inch front tires
24.5-inch crop clearance
52-80-inch adjustable tread

Model D-12 Series II Industrial (G149 engine) Standard Features
11.2x24-inch four-ply industrial rear tires
6.00x16-inch front tires
Heavy-duty, nonadjustable wide front axle
Heavy-duty clutch
Three-point hitch (draft responsive)
Power steering

Allis-Chalmers Models I-40 and I-400

Nebraska test number	not tested
Location of serial number	left, front end of torque housing
Location of engine number	left side of block rear of carburetor
Total production (I-40)	554
Total production (I-400)	748
Production years	
Model I-40	1964–1966
Model I-400	1966–1968

Specifications

Mechanically, the I-40 and I-400 models were about the same as the D-10 Series II tractors. During 1966, the I-40 was renamed the I-400 with little change.

These tractors were painted yellow and had box-shaped grilles to distinguish them from agricultural models. Several of these tractors were sold with a 0.50- or 0.75-yard loader with a 2,500-pound lift. Also a 10- or 13-foot reach backhoe attachment was offered with the loader versions.

Weight (I-40 and I-400)	2,936 pounds
Price	
I-40	$3,120 in 1966
I-400	$3,755 in 1966

Options

Shuttle clutch (changes direction of all gears)
Two-range transmission
Rear wheel weights
PTO/belt pulley assembly
Three-point hitch

Model I-40 and I-400 Standard Features

Hydrostatic power steering
Deluxe seat
Industrial yellow paint
Heavy-duty, fixed-tread front axle
Heavy-duty, fixed-tread rear wheel rims (62-inch wheel tread)
6.00x16- or 7.50x16-inch front tires
12.4x24- or 14.9x24-inch six-ply industrial rear tires

Production History (I-40 Models)

Year	Beginning number
1964	1055
1965	not known
1966	not known
Ending serial number	1608

Production History (I-400 Models)

Year	Beginning number
1966	1003
1967	1281
1968	1495
Ending serial number	1750

Allis-Chalmers Model D-15, Series I (total production 7,169)

Nebraska test numbers	795/796/797
Serial numbers (all D-15 models)	1001–25419
Serial numbers (Series I models)	1001–8169
Location of serial number	left, front side of torque housing
Location of engine number	left side of block
Production years (all D-15 models)	1960–1968
Production years (Series I models)	1960–1962
Total production (all D-15 models)	19,588
Total production (Series I models)	7,169

Engine
- Gasoline and propane — Allis-Chalmers vertical, four-cylinder I-head
- Diesel — Allis-Chalmers vertical, four-cylinder injected

Bore and stroke
- Gasoline and LPG — 3.5x3.875 inches
- Diesel — 3.5625x4.375 inches

Rated rpm (all versions) — 2,000

Displacement
- Gasoline and LPG — 149 cubic inches
- Diesel — 175 cubic inches

Compression ratio
- Gasoline — 7.75:1
- LPG — 8.9:1
- Diesel — 15.5:1

Engine ratings
- Gasoline (test no. 795)
  - Drawbar — 35.33 horsepower
  - PTO/belt — 40.00 horsepower
  - Maximum pull — 5,606 pounds
- LPG (test no. 797)
  - Drawbar — 33.22 horsepower
  - PTO/belt — 37.44 horsepower
  - Maximum pull — 5,668 pounds
- Diesel (test no. 796)
  - Drawbar — 33.32 horsepower
  - PTO/belt — 36.51 horsepower
  - Maximum pull — 5,737 pounds

Speed
- D-15 Series I except High-Clearance
- High-range
  - First gear — 2.7 mph
  - Second gear — 4.7 mph
  - Third gear — 6.1 mph
  - Fourth gear — 15.3 mph
  - Reverse — 4.7 mph
- Low-range (Power-Director)
  - First gear — 1.9 mph
  - Second gear — 3.3 mph

Third gear	4.3 mph
Fourth gear	10.9 mph
Reverse	3.3 mph

D-15 Series I High-Clearance Models

High-range

First gear	3.2 mph
Second gear	4.6 mph
Third gear	7.1 mph
Fourth gear	17.9 mph
Reverse	5.6 mph

Low-range (Power-Director)

First gear	2.0 mph
Second gear	3.6 mph
Third gear	5.7 mph
Fourth gear	11.6 mph
Reverse	3.6 mph

Length	130.19 inches
Rear tread	54 to 80 inches
Height	80.19 inches

Weight

Gasoline	3,985 pounds
LPG	4,036 pounds
Diesel	4,220 pounds

Carburetor

Gasoline	Marvel-Schebler TSX815, TSX844, or TSX869
LPG	Ensign Mg 1
Diesel injector pump	Roosa-Master
Ignition (gasoline and LPG)	Delco-Remy 1112607
Air cleaner	Donaldson (oil)
Front tire	6.00x16 inches
Rear tire	12.4x26 inches
Fuel tank capacity (gasoline and diesel)	14 gallons
LPG tank capacity (80 percent usable volume)	15.8 gallons
Cooling capacity	9 quarts
Crankcase oil capacity	4 quarts
Transmission oil capacity	14.5 quarts
Final drive oil capacity (each)	0.75 quarts

Tune-up

Firing order

Gasoline and LPG	1-2-4-3
Diesel	1-3-4-2

Spark plug used

Gasoline	Champion J-11
LPG	Champion J-3

Spark plug gap

Gasoline	0.025 inches
LPG	0.020 inches

Ignition point gap (gasoline and LPG)   0.022 inches
Timing (marks on flywheel or
crankshaft pulley)
    Nondiesel at 1,750 rpm   25 degrees BTDC
    Diesel (pump no. DBGFC429-1AF)   22 degrees BTDC
    Diesel (pump no. DBGFC429-5AF)   22 degrees BTDC
    Diesel (pump no. DGFCL629-12A)   23 degrees BTDC
    Diesel (pump no. DBGFC637-12AJ)   16 degrees BTDC
    Diesel (pump no. DBGFC637-14AJ)   16 degrees BTDC
    Diesel (pump no. DBGFC637-17AJ)   16 degrees BTDC
    Diesel (pump no. DBGFC637-32AJ)   16 degrees BTDC
Prices
    Gasoline (narrow, dual front axle) $3,175 in 1962
    LPG (narrow, dual front axle) $3,504 in 1962
    Diesel (narrow, dual front axle) $3,935 in 1962
Paint
The tractor is painted Persian Orange no. 2, and the grille and wheels are painted
cream color with silver rims.

Options
Power-Director (two-range speed control)
Shuttle clutch
Front wheel weights
Rear wheel weights (58-pound quarter sections)
Power steering
6.56-inch wide by 9-inch diameter belt pulley assembly
Operation meter (hours, PTO rpm, engine rpm, mph)
Orchard shielding

Comments
    The D-15 was basically a continuation of the earlier D-14 model.
    In the unofficial Series I, the tractors were built in the following configurations
and numbers:
Model D-15 Series I (gasoline, narrow)   897 units built
Model D-15 Series I (gasoline, Roll-Shift) 5,315 units built
Model D-15 Series I (diesel, narrow)   83 units built
Model D-15 Series I (diesel, Roll-Shift)   855 units built
Model D-15 Series I (diesel, Grove)   18 units built

Model D-15 Series I Nondiesel Standard Features
Dual, narrow front axle
Fenders
12-volt Delco-Remy 1107758 starter plus lights
PTO assembly (666 rpm)
Traction-Booster draft system

Model D-15 Series I Diesel Standard Features
Dual, narrow front axle
Fenders
12-volt Delco-Remy 1107502 starter plus lights
PTO assembly (666 rpm)
Traction-Booster draft system

Model D-15 Series I Industrial Standard Features
Heavy-duty, fixed-tread wide front axle
Power steering
Fenders
12-volt Delco-Remy starter plus lights
12.4x26-inch four-ply industrial rear tires
7.50x16-inch front tires
Drawbar
Shuttle clutch (reverses direction of all gears)

Model D-15 Series I High-Clearance Standard Features
Dual, narrow front axle
11.2x38-inch four-ply rear tires
Fenders
12-volt Delco-Remy starter plus lights
28.5-inch crop clearance

Model D-15 Series I Grove Standard Features
Adjustable wide front axle with undermount headlights
Rear wheel citrus fenders and operator screen guard
26-inch turf tires
12-volt Delco-Remy starter plus lights
Downward exhaust

Production History (all D-15 models)

Year	Beginning number
1960	1001
1961	1900
1962	6470
1963	13001
1964	16928
1965	19681
1966	21375
1967	23734
1968	25127
Ending serial number	25419

Allis-Chalmers Model D-15, Series II (total production 12,419)

Nebraska test numbers	837 and 838
Serial numbers (all D-15 models)	1001–25419
Serial numbers (Series II models)	13001–25419
Location of serial number	left, front side of torque housing
Location of engine number	left side of block
Production years (all D-15 models)	1960–1968
Production years (Series II models)	1963–1968
Total production (all D-15 models)	19,588
Total production (Series II models)	12,419
Engine	Allis-Chalmers vertical, four-cylinder I-head

Bore and stroke
  Gasoline and LPG   3.625x3.875 inches
  Diesel   3.5625x4.375 inches
Rated rpm (all versions)   2,000
Displacement
  Gasoline and LPG   160 cubic inches
  Diesel   175 cubic inches
Compression ratio
  Gasoline   7.75:1
  LPG   8.9:1
  Diesel   15.5:1
Engine ratings
  Gasoline (test no. 837)
    Drawbar   38.33 horsepower
    PTO/ belt   46.18 horsepower
    Maximum pull   6,157 pounds
  LPG (test no. 838)
    Drawbar   36.02 horsepower
    PTO/belt   43.55 horsepower
    Maximum pull   6,447 pounds
  Diesel (test no. 796)
    Drawbar   33.32 horsepower
    PTO/belt   36.51 horsepower
    Maximum pull   5,737 pounds
Speed
  D-15 Series II models except High-Clearance
  High-range
    First gear   2.7 mph
    Second gear   4.7 mph
    Third gear   6.1 mph
    Fourth gear   15.3 mph
    Reverse   4.7 mph
  Low-range (Power-Director)
    First gear   1.8 mph
    Second gear   3.1 mph
    Third gear   4.8 mph
    Fourth gear   9.9 mph
    Reverse   3.1 mph
  D-15 Series II High-Clearance
  High-range
    First gear   3.2 mph
    Second gear   4.6 mph
    Third gear   7.1 mph
    Fourth gear   17.9 mph
    Reverse   5.6 mph
  Low-range (Power-Director)
    First gear   2.0 mph
    Second gear   3.6 mph
    Third gear   5.7 mph
    Fourth gear   11.6 mph
    Reverse   3.6 mph

Length	130.19 inches
Rear tread	54–80 inches
Height	80.19 inches
Weight	
Gasoline	4,025 pounds
LPG	4,090 pounds
Diesel	4,220 pounds
Carburetor	
Gasoline	Marvel-Schebler TSX815, TSX844, or TSX869
LPG	Ensign Mg 1
Diesel injector pump	Roosa-Master
Ignition (gasoline and LPG)	Delco-Remy 1112607
Air cleaner	dry element
Front tire	6.00x16 inches
Rear tire	12.4x26 inches
Fuel tank capacity (gasoline and diesel)	14.0 gallons
LPG tank capacity (80 percent usable volume)	15.8 gallons
Cooling capacity	9 quarts
Crankcase oil capacity	4 quarts
Transmission oil capacity	14.5 quarts
Final drive oil capacity (each)	0.75 quarts
Tune-up	
Firing order	
Gasoline and LPG	1-2-4-3
Diesel	1-3-4-2
Spark plug used	
Gasoline	Champion J-8
LPG	Champion J-3
Spark plug gap	
Gasoline	0.025 inches
LPG	0.020 inches
Ignition point gap (gasoline and LPG)	0.022 inches
Timing (marks on flywheel or crankshaft pulley)	
Nondiesel models at 1,750 rpm	25 degrees BTDC
Diesel (pump no. DBGFC429-1AF)	22 degrees BTDC
Diesel (pump no. DBGFC429-5AF)	22 degrees BTDC
Diesel (pump no. DGFCL629-12A)	23 degrees BTDC
Diesel (pump no. DBGFC637-12AJ)	16 degrees BTDC
Diesel (pump no. DBGFC637-17AJ)	16 degrees BTDC
Diesel (pump no. DBGFC637-32AJ)	16 degrees BTDC
Price (Model D-15 Series II)	
Gasoline (Roll-Shift front axle)	$4,180 in 1967
LPG (Roll-Shift front axle)	$4,509 in 1967
Diesel (Roll-Shift front axle)	$4,852 in 1967
Paint	

The tractor is painted Persian Orange no. 2 and the grille and wheels are painted cream with silver rims. The hood transfers on the Series II model are longer than ones on the Series I model. Series II is labeled on the side of the fuel tank.

Options
Dual, narrow front axle
Single front wheel (9.00x10-inch tire)
Front wheel weights (90 pounds each)
Rear wheel weights (58-pound quarter sections)
Power steering
6.56-inch wide by 9-inch diameter belt pulley (1,384 rpm)
Power-Director (two-range speed control)
Orchard shielding

Comments
　　Series II models had the headlights mounted on the fenders and had a black oval muffler to replace the silver cylindrical-type on Series I models.
　　Industrial models were changed in 1965 with heavy-duty, box-shaped grilles. The company designated these tractors the Model I-60 in 1965 and redesignated them as the Model I-600 in 1966.

Model D-15 Series II Nondiesel Standard Features
12-volt Delco-Remy 1107758 starter plus lights
PTO assembly (666 rpm)
12.4x26-inch rear tires and fenders
21.1875-inch crop clearance (adjustable wide front axle)
54- to 80-inch rear tread
Shipping weight of 4,460 pounds

Model D-15 Series II Diesel Standard Features
12-volt Delco-Remy 1107502 starter plus lights
PTO assembly (666 rpm)
12.4x26-inch rear tires and fenders
21.1875-inch crop clearance
54- to 80-inch rear tread
Shipping weight of 4,525 pounds

Model D-15 Series II High-Clearance Standard Features
12-volt Delco-Remy 1107758 starter (nondiesel) plus lights
PTO assembly (666 rpm)
11.2x38-inch rear tires and fenders
25.5-inch crop clearance (adjustable wide front axle)
58.375- to 100.875-inch rear tread
Shipping weight of 4,525 pounds (gasoline)

Model D-15 Series II Grove (Cage Type) Standard Features
Diesel engine
12-volt Delco-Remy 1107502 starter
Full rear fenders and mesh engine surround tip up for access
Low operator seat
18.4x26-inch rear turf tires
Downward exhaust
Lights (two headlights in front of lower grille)
70-inch overall height

Allis-Chalmers Models I-60 and I-600

Nebraska test number	not tested
Location of serial number	left, front side of torque housing
Location of engine number	left side of block
Total production (I-60)	1,336
Total production (I-600)	2,055
Production years	
Model I-60	1965–1966
Model I-600	1966–1968

Specifications

Mechanically, the I-60 and I-600 models were basically the same as the D-15 Series II tractor. The I-60 was renamed the Model I-600 in 1966 with little change.

These tractors were painted yellow with a box-shaped grille to distinguish them from agricultural models. Allis-Chalmers sold many of these tractors with a 0.75- or 0.875-yard front loader. Others came with a 15-foot backhoe on the loader tractor. Forklift versions were made with choice of a 12- or 21-foot reach and 48-inch forks. Mowers, power sweepers, and hydraulic hammers were just a few of the many attachments sold with these industrial tractors.

Weight

I-60 (gasoline)	3,371 pounds
I-60 (diesel)	3,443 pounds
I-600 (gasoline)	4,112 pounds
I-600 (diesel)	4,364 pounds

Price

I-60 (gasoline)	$3,967 in 1966
I-60 (diesel)	$4,567 in 1966
I-600 (gasoline)	$4,564 in 1967
I-600 (diesel)	$5,188 in 1967

Models I-60 and I-600 (Industrial) Standard Features

Hydrostatic power steering
Gasoline or diesel engine
Shuttle clutch
Front-mounted 15.5-gpm hydraulic pump (two-spool valve)
Heavy-duty clutch (I-600)
Industrial yellow paint
12.4x24- or 16.9x24-inch rear tires (rims not Power-Shift)
6.00x16- or 7.5x16-inch front tires
Box-shaped grille
Deluxe seat
Heavy-duty, fixed-tread front axle

Production History (I-60 Models)

Year	Beginning number
1965	1005
1966	not known
Ending serial number	2340

Production History (I-600 models)

Year	Beginning number

1966	1002
1967	1747
1968	2709
Ending serial number	3056

Allis-Chalmers Model D-19 (total production 10,597)

Nebraska test numbers	810/811/814
Serial numbers	1001–16266
Location of serial number	top of rear primary cast housing under seat
Location of engine number	left side of block at top
Production years	1961–1964
Total production	10,597
Engine (all D-19 models)	Allis-Chalmers vertical six-cylinder I-head
Bore and stroke (all D-19 models)	3.625x4.375 inches
Rated rpm (all D-19 models)	2,000
Displacement (all D-19 models)	262 cubic inches
Compression ratio	
Gasoline	8.0:1
LPG	9.65:1
Diesel (prior to engine no. 014419)	14.0:1
Diesel (engine no 014419 and up)	15.0:1
Engine ratings	
Gasoline (test no. 810)	
Drawbar	63.91 horsepower
PTO/belt	71.54 horsepower
Maximum pull	8,587 pounds
LPG (test no. 814)	
Drawbar	58.29 horsepower
PTO/belt	66.19 horsepower
Maximum pull	8,674 pounds
Diesel (test no. 811)	
Drawbar	62.05 horsepower
PTO/belt	66.92 horsepower
Maximum pull	8,459 pounds
Speed (regular and High-Clearance models)	
High-range	
First gear	3.0 mph
Second gear	4.1 mph
Third gear	6.3 mph
Fourth gear	13.9 mph
Reverse	4.0 mph
Low-range (Power-Director)	
First gear	1.9 mph
Second gear	3.1 mph
Third gear	4.7 mph
Fourth gear	9.0 mph
Reverse	2.6 mph

Wheelbase	102.375 inches
Rear tread	
Power-Shift wheels	60–88 inches
Without Power-Shift wheels	60–80 inches
Height (nondiesel, wide front)	84.375 inches
Weight	
Gasoline	6,645 pounds
LPG	6,785 pounds
Diesel	6,835 pounds
Carburetor	
Gasoline	Marvel-Schebler TSX-848
LPG	Ensign XG
Diesel injector pump	Roosa-Master
Ignition (distributor)	Delco-Remy 1112615
Air cleaner	dry element
Front tire	6.50x16 or 7.50x16 inches
Rear tire	18.4x34 or 15.5x38 inches
Fuel tank capacity (gasoline and diesel)	23 gallons
Cooling capacity	
Nondiesel models	16 quarts
Diesel models	17 quarts
Crankcase oil capacity (all versions)	7 quarts
Transmission and differential oil capacity	32 quarts
Power-Director and hydraulic oil capacity	22 quarts
Final drive oil capacity (each)	8 quarts
Tune-up	
Firing order (all D-19 models)	1-5-3-6-2-4
Spark plug used	
Gasoline	Champion N8
LPG	Champion N3
Spark plug gap	0.025 inches
Ignition point gap	0.022 inches
Timing (advanced for nondiesel models)	25 degrees BTDC (crankshaft pulley)
Timing (diesel injection, static, marks on crankshaft pulley)	
Pump no. 4513709	16 degrees BTDC
Pump no. 4514017	16 degrees BTDC
Pump no. 4514557	20 degrees BTDC
Pump no. 4514756	20 degrees BTDC
Price	
Model D-19 (gasoline, tricycle)	$5,305 in 1964
Model D-19 (gasoline, Roll-Shift)	$5,443 in 1964
Model D-19 (gasoline, Rice)	$5,888 in 1964
Model D-19 (gasoline, High-Clearance)	$6,302 in 1964
Model D-19 (diesel option)	add $775 in 1964
Model D-19 (LPG option)	add $360 in 1964

Paint
The tractor is Persian Orange no. 2 and the grille and wheels are cream-colored with silver wheel rims.

Options
Single front wheel style (9.00x10-inch tire)
Roll-Shift adjustable wide front axle
Front or rear wheel weights
Three-point or Snap-Coupler hitch
Traction-Booster drawbar
Three-spool hydraulic control valve
6.56-inch wide by 9-inch diameter belt pulley (1,678 rpm)
38-inch rear tires
Power-Shift rear wheel rims

Comments
This five-plow tractor was the first model to have power steering as a standard feature.
At diesel engine no. D1499, the pistons no longer had valve recesses in them; also the head, valves, camshaft, and injectors were changed. The newer valves had a smaller diameter and the newer head was less apt to crack. The camshaft was redesigned for easier starting.

Model D-19 Standard Features
Fenders
Dual wheel, tricycle front axle
Power-Director (two-range speed control)
Power steering
12-volt Delco-Remy 1107235 starter (gasoline models)
12-volt Delco-Remy 1113152 starter (diesel models)
Live PTO assembly (612 rpm)
Lights
Diesel engine has a Thompson turbocharger as standard equipment
27-inch ground clearance (tricycle)

Model D-19 High-Clearance Standard Features
Available in gasoline, propane, and diesel versions
Rear tread of 60–90 inches
7.50x20-inch front tires (9.00x10-inch single front tire)
Power-Director (two-range speed control)
Power steering
15.5x38-inch six-ply rear tires
12-volt Delco-Remy starter plus lights
Overall height of 97.6875 inches (nondiesel)
Overall height of 102.3125 inches (diesel)
37-inch ground clearance (wide front and tricycle)
Shipping weight of 7,000 pounds (nondiesel)
Shipping weight of 6,820 pounds (diesel)
Speeds rated the same as regular D-19 models
1,385 diesel versions were built (gasoline total not known)

Model D-19 Rice Tractor Standard Features
Same features as the standard model except the following:
23.1x26-inch rear rice tires on standard rims
Mud shields (below fenders)
Roll-Shift adjustable wide front axle with 7.50x16-inch tires

Production History (all D-19 Models)

Year	Beginning number
1961	1001
1962	1250-7331
1963	12001
1964	14945
Ending serial number	16266

Allis-Chalmers Model ED-40 (Great Britain)

Nebraska test number	not tested
Serial numbers	1001–?
Location of serial number	top left side of transmission case
Location of engine number	on engine block under forward part of exhaust manifold
Production years	1960–1966
Total production	4,000 (estimate)
Engine	Standard-Ricardo vertical, four-cylinder diesel
Bore and stroke	3.3125x4.0 inches
Rated rpm	
Prior to July 1963	2,000
July 1963 and after	2,250
Displacement	137.89 cubic inches
Fuel	diesel
Compression ratio	20:1
Engine ratings (factory)	
Engine (brake)	
Prior to July 1963	37 horsepower
July 1963 and after	41 horsepower
PTO/belt (July 1963 and after)	33.7 horsepower
Speed (two-range transmission)	
High-range	
First gear	2.47 mph
Second gear	3.94 mph
Third gear	6.52 mph
Fourth gear	16.4 mph
Reverse	5.1 mph
Low-range	
First gear	1.22 mph
Second gear	1.94 mph
Third gear	3.23 mph
Fourth gear	8.14 mph
Reverse	2.52 mph

Length	114 inches
Tread width	48–72 inches
Height	68 inches
Weight (shipping)	3,584 pounds
Diesel injector pump	CAV
Air cleaner	oil type
Front tire	6.00x16 inches
Rear tire	11x28 inches
Fuel tank capacity	11.75 gallons
Cooling capacity	2.128 gallons
Crankcase oil capacity	6 quarts
Transmission oil capacity	27 quarts
Tune-up	
Firing order	1-3-4-2
Injection timing (DPA 3243390)	13 degrees BTDC
Price (standard model)	£636 in 1963
Paint	Persian Orange no. 2

Options
Power-adjustable rear wheels
10-inch diameter belt pulley
Lighting equipment and horn
Stabilizer chains for three-point lift
Swinging drawbar frame with either short or long drawbar
Trailer pick up hook (hydraulic rear hook)
Category 2, three-point conversion kit
Handbrake
Exhaust pipe extension
Combined oil and temperature gauge
Radiator shutters
Front and rear wheel weights

Comments
   The ED-40 was made in Essendine, England, and was introduced in November 1960 starting with serial number 1001.
   The Lucas RB108 37229J voltage regulator was changed at 1960 serial number 1005 and up to a Lucas RB108 37228H regulator.
   The Depthomatic draft system with a two-lever control was introduced at 1963 serial number 3310.
   About 450 ED-40 tractors were imported to the eastern United States in 1964. Problems with broken lift-arm housings from the hydraulic lift system over-extending caused a bad reputation in the United States, even though limiting chains were added to prevent further problems. An improved system with a single control and a changeover lever for depth and position was used beginning with 1966 serial number 4874. This newer Depthomatic system had two-way draft sensing. A hydraulic full-flow pressure filter was added at 1966 serial number 4935.
   Production figures have not been found, but the serial numbers imply that somewhere around 4,000 units were produced.

Model ED-40 Standard Features
4.00x19-inch front & 10x28-inch rear tires
Adjustable wide front axle

Depthomatic hydraulic draft system
Plessey brand live hydraulic pump (5.35 gallons per minute)
Three governed engine speeds, 800/1,700/2,250 rpm
Category 1, three-point hitch (2,500-pound lift capacity)
PTO assembly (547 rpm)
High- and low-range four-speed transmission
Engine heater plugs (serial no. 1229 and up)
12-volt Lucas M45G starter
Six-blade radiator fan and 10-inch single plate master clutch (dry)

Model ED-40 Deluxe Standard Features

Same features as standard model plus the following:
6.00x16-inch front and 10x28-inch rear tires
Live PTO assembly (547 rpm)
Differential lock
Tractormeter
Fuel level gauge (mechanical)

Model ED-40 Super Deluxe Standard Features

Same features as the Deluxe model plus the following:
6.00x16-inch front and 11x28-inch rear tires
12-volt lights and horn
Swinging drawbar frame with short drawbar

Allis-Chalmers Model D-21, Series I (total production 1,129)

Nebraska test number	855
Serial numbers (all D-21 models)	1001–4609
Serial numbers (Series I models)	1001–2129
Location of serial number	left, front side of torque housing on flange
Location of engine number	left side of block at upper, rear corner
Production years (all D-21 models)	1963–1969
Production years (Series I models)	1963–1965
Total production (all D-21 models)	3,538
Total production (Series I models)	1,129
Engine	Allis-Chalmers vertical, six-cylinder diesel
Bore and stroke	4.25x5.0 inches
Rated rpm	2,200
Displacement	426 cubic inches
Compression ratio	16.0:1
Engine ratings	
Drawbar	93.09 horsepower
PTO	103.06 horsepower
Maximum pull	14,840 pounds
Speed	
High-range	

108

First gear	2.4 mph
Second gear	4.4 mph
Third gear	8.7 mph
Fourth gear	16.2 mph
Reverse	6.8 mph
Low-range	
First gear	1.6 mph
Second gear	3.4 mph
Third gear	5.8 mph
Fourth gear	12.5 mph
Reverse	1.8 mph
Length	160.625 inches
Rear tread	68–88 inches
Height (overall)	106.5625 inches
Height (to top of hood)	71.75 inches
Weight	10,745 pounds
Diesel injector pump	Roosa-Master
Air cleaner	dry element
Front tire	11.00x16 inches
Rear tire	18.4x34 inches
Fuel tank capacity	52 gallons
Cooling capacity	21 quarts
Crankcase oil capacity	12 quarts
Transmission oil capacity	87 quarts
Tune-up	
Firing order	1-5-3-6-2-4
Timing (static)	34 degrees BTDC (pulley) timing lines on cam and governor plate should line up with each other
Price	
D-21	$10,290 in 1965
D-21 Industrial	$8,901 in 1965
Paint	

The tractor is painted Persian Orange no. 2 and the grille and wheels are a cream color with silver-colored wheel rims. Industrial models were usually painted yellow.

Options
24.5x32-inch rear tires (standard or rice tread)
18.4x34-inch rear tires (rice tread)
18.4x38-inch rear tires (standard or rice tread)
15.5x38-inch rear tires (standard tread)
28.1x32-inch rear tires (10-ply diamond tread)
Dual rear wheels (for 18.4x34- or 18.4x38-inch tires)
11x16-inch front tires
Front-end weight set (three weights at 367 pounds total)
Rear wheel weights (sectional six-piece at 77 pounds each)
Rear wheel weights for 34- or 38-inch wheels (450-pound discs)
Rear wheel weights for 32-inch wheels (280-pound discs)
Two extra 12-volt batteries (total of four)
Cold weather starting aid
Three-point hitch (with category-2 or -3 sway blocks)

Traction-Booster system and Traction-Booster drawbar
Hydraulic system (one- or three-spool valve)
Operation meter
Deluxe or Super Deluxe (armchair) seat
Air intake extension
Filter service indicator (air filter)

Comments
This was the first Allis-Chalmers farm tractor rated over 100 horsepower.
Prior to serial number 1964, the 14-inch clutch assembly had 15 springs. At serial number 1964 and up, the clutch plate was changed to ceramic and the assembly had 12 springs.

Model D-21 Series I Standard Features
18.4x34-inch rear tires with large fenders
Tilt-steering with tilt-dash (four-position)
Live PTO and hydraulics
Hydrostatic power steering
Adjustable wide front axle (60- to 80-inch front tread)
Power-Director (two-range speed control)
Swinging roller-type drawbar
Adjustable contoured metal seat

Model D-21 Industrial Series I Standard Features
24.5x32-inch rear tires (eight-ply) with large fenders
Tilt-steering with tilt dash (four-position)
Power steering
Power-Director (two-range speed control)
Swinging roller-type drawbar
Deluxe seat

Production History (all D-21 models)

Year	Beginning number
1963	1001
1964	1417
1965	2079
1966	2408
1967	2863
1968	3777
1969	4498
Ending serial number	4609

Allis-Chalmers Model D-21, Series II
(total production 2,409)

Nebraska test number	904
Serial numbers (all D-21 models)	1001–4609
Serial numbers (Series II models)	2201–4609
Location of serial number	left, front side of torque housing on flange
Location of engine number	left side of block at upper, rear corner
Production years (all D-21 models)	1963–1969
Production years (Series II models)	1965–1969
Total production (all D-21 models)	3,538
Total production (Series II models)	2,409
Engine	Allis-Chalmers vertical, six-cylinder diesel
Bore and stroke	4.25x5.0 inches
Rated rpm	2,200
Displacement	426 cubic inches
Compression ratio	16.0:1
Engine ratings	
Drawbar	116.41 horsepower
PTO	127.75 horsepower
Maximum pull	15,261 pounds
Speed	
High-range	
First gear	2.4 mph
Second gear	4.4 mph
Third gear	8.7 mph
Fourth gear	16.2 mph
Reverse	6.8 mph
Low-range	
First gear	1.6 mph
Second gear	3.4 mph
Third gear	5.8 mph
Fourth gear	12.5 mph
Reverse	1.8 mph
Length	160.625 inches
Rear tread	68–88 inches
Height (to top of hood)	71.75 inches
Height (overall)	105.25 inches
Weight	10,675 pounds
Diesel injector pump	Roosa-Master
Air cleaner	dry element
Front tire	11.00x16 inches
Rear tire	24.5x32 inches
Fuel tank capacity	52 gallons
Cooling capacity	21 quarts
Crankcase oil capacity	12 quarts
Transmission oil capacity	87 quarts
Tune-up	
Firing order	1-5-3-6-2-4

| Timing (static) | 34 degrees BTDC (pulley) timing lines on the cam and governor plate should line up with each other |

Price
  D-21 $10,764 in 1967
  D-21 Industrial (no hydraulics) $10,092 in 1967
Paint

The tractor is painted Persian Orange no. 2 and the grille and wheels are a cream color with silver-colored wheel rims.

The industrial version was usually painted yellow.

Options

24.5x32-inch rear tires (standard or rice tread)
18.4x34-inch rear tires (rice tread)
18.4x38-inch rear tires (standard or rice tread)
15.5x38-inch rear tires (standard tread)
28.1x32-inch rear tires (10-ply diamond tread)
Dual rear wheels (for 18.4x34- or 18.4x38-inch tires)
11x16-inch front tires
Front-end weight set (three weights at 367 pounds total)
Rear wheel weights (sectional six-piece at 77 pounds each)
Rear wheel weights for 34- or 38-inch wheels (450-pound discs)
Rear wheel weights for 32-inch wheels (280-pound discs)
Two extra 12-volt batteries (total of four)
Cold weather starting aid
Three-point hitch (with category-2 or -3 sway blocks)
Traction-Booster system
Traction-Booster drawbar
Hydraulic system (one- or three-spool valve)
Operation meter
Deluxe or Super Deluxe (armchair) seat
Air intake extension
Air filter service indicator

Comments

   The Series II, D-21 engine was almost the same as the Series I, except for the added feature of a turbocharger and related parts.

Model D-21 Series II Standard Features

Turbocharger (Thompson brand)
Large fenders
Tilt steering with tilt dash (four-position)
Live PTO (1,000 rpm) and hydraulics
Hydrostatic power steering
Adjustable wide front axle (60- to 80-inch front tread)
Power-Director (two-range speed control)
Swinging roller-type drawbar
Adjustable contoured metal seat

Model D-21 Industrial Series II Standard Features

Turbocharger (Thompson brand)
18.4x34-inch rear tires with large fenders
Tilt steering with tilt dash (four-position)
Adjustable wide front axle and hydrostatic power steering
Power-Director (two-range speed control)
Swinging roller-type drawbar
Deluxe seat

At 103.06 PTO horsepower, the D-21 Series I tractor was considered a seven-plow tractor. With a four-position tilt steering wheel and hydrostatic steering, this immense tractor was designed with comfort in mind.

Monarch 50 Crawler

Allis-Chalmers inherited the Model H-50 crawler when it purchased the Monarch Tractor Company in 1928. Allis-Chalmers added its diamond logo to the improved version and renamed it the Model 50 in 1929. This chain-drive crawler was quickly antiquated by more advanced crawlers with faster gearing and more attractive pricing. Production of this model ended in 1931.

Allis-Chalmers Monarch 50 Crawler (total production 2,000)

Nebraska test numbers	147 and 179
Serial numbers	60298–62297
Location of serial number	front frame and on dash instruction plate
Location of engine number	
Stearns engine	left side of block near clutch housing
Allis-Chalmers engine	left side of block near center
Production years	1928–1931
Total production (all Monarch 50 models)	2,000
Total production (Stearns engine)	1,399
Total production (Allis-Chalmers engine)	601

Engine
    Prior to serial no. 61698   Stearns four-cylinder vertical
                                          I-head
    1930 serial no. 61698 and up   Allis-Chalmers four-cylinder
                                          vertical I-head

Bore and stroke	
Stearns engine	5.125x6.5 inches
Allis-Chalmers engine	5.25x6.5 inches
Rated rpm (all Monarch 50 models)	1,000
Displacement	
Stearns engine	536 cubic inches
Allis-Chalmers engine	562.8 cubic inches
Fuel	gasoline
Engine ratings (Stearns engine, test no. 147)	
Drawbar	50.55 horsepower
PTO/belt	not tested
Maximum pull	10,537 pounds
Engine ratings (Allis-Chalmers engine, test no. 179)	
Drawbar	53.28 horsepower
PTO/belt	62.18 horsepower
Maximum pull	10,573 pounds
Speed	
Standard 9-tooth chain drive sprockets	
First gear	1.81 mph
Second gear	2.74 mph
Third gear	3.96 mph
Reverse	2.07 mph
Optional 8-tooth chain drive sprockets	
First gear	1.61 mph
Second gear	2.44 mph
Third gear	3.52 mph
Reverse	1.84 mph
Optional 10-tooth chain drive sprockets	
First gear	2.01 mph
Second gear	3.04 mph
Third gear	4.40 mph
Reverse	2.30 mph
Optional 11-tooth chain drive sprockets	
First gear	2.21 mph
Second gear	3.35 mph
Third gear	4.84 mph
Reverse	2.53 mph
Length	127.81 inches
Standard track gauge	57 inches
Height (to top of radiator)	67.375 inches
Height (to top of cab)	89.81 inches
Weight	15,100 pounds

Carburetor
  Stearns engine (prior to serial
    no. 61059)   Zenith 77 (1.75-inch)
  Stearns engine (serial no. 61059–
    61697)   Zenith 76 (1.5-inch)
  Allis-Chalmers engine   Zenith C6 (1.5-inch)
Ignition
  Monarch 50 prior to serial
    no. 61059   American Bosch ZR4
  Monarch 50 at serial no. 61059
    and up   Eisemann GV-4
Air cleaner
  Monarch 50 prior to serial _
    no. 61059   Pomona 638 (oil)
  Monarch 50 serial no. 61059–
    61697   Pomona 1021 (oil)
  Monarch 50 serial no. 61698
    and up   Allis-Chalmers (dry)
Standard track shoe width   13 inches
Number of shoes per track   32
Rollers per side   5
Fuel tank capacity   35 gallons
Cooling capacity   8 gallons
Crankcase oil capacity
  Stearns engine   12 quarts
  Allis-Chalmers engine   14 quarts
Transmission oil capacity   10 quarts
Final drive oil capacity (each side)
  Semi-enclosed (prior to serial
    no. 60601)   1 quart
  Oil tight (serial no. 60601 and up)   8 quarts
Tune-up
  Firing order   1-3-4-2
  Spark plug used (Stearns
    engine)   7/8-inch extended
  Spark plug used
    (Allis-Chalmers engine)   Champion W-10
  Spark plug gap   0.025 inches
  Ignition point gap   0.12 inches
  Timing (Allis-Chalmers engine)   26 degrees BTDC
Price
  Monarch 50 $3,625 in 1928
  Monarch 50 $3,540 in 1929
Paint (1929 and after)   Persian Orange

Options
8-, 10-, or 11-tooth chain drive sprockets (9-tooth standard)
Low-speed reverse gearing (discontinued at serial no. 60898 and up)
Regular, open, or smooth 13-inch grousers (steel or manganese)
15-, 18-, and 22-inch grousers (Hillside model)
12.5-inch diameter by 9.5-inch wide belt pulley (950 rpm)

PTO (1,000 rpm, 30 inches above ground)
Grille shield and engine shield
Crankcase guard
Auto-Lite ML4123 (barrel-mount) or ML4147 (flange-mount) starter
Cab curtains (four sides) or an enclosed cab
Hydraulic pump (gear type) and valve assembly
Odometer (Veeder brand, hub type)
Underhood Pomona 821 air cleaner (serial nos. 60298–61058 only)
Dust-proof transmission cover equipment (shaft and lever seals)
Electric lights (standard on serial no. 61697 and up)
Headlight guards (logging)

Comments
    Allis-Chalmers arranged to purchase the languishing Monarch Tractor Com-
pany at the end of February 1928 for $500,000. Allis-Chalmers announced this
acquisition on April 2.
    The Monarch 50 has a 44-link Baldwin chain from each steering clutch
assembly to each track drive sprocket assembly. The early-type chain housings
were semi-enclosed and had wool wick-type chain lubricators. The chain housings were improved at 1928 serial number 60601 with oil-tight seals for oil-
bath lubrication. Replacing the 9-tooth chain drive sprockets with 8-, 10-, or
11-tooth sprockets would change speeds of the crawler.
    A five-inch track equalizer beam replaced a four-inch beam starting at 1929
serial number 60698 and up.
    A hollow-tooth track drive sprocket replaced the pin-type starting at 1929
serial number 61348. A double-tooth sprocket replaced the hollow-tooth
sprocket starting at 1931 serial number 62171 until the end of production.
    The Stearns engine had changes to the block, manifolds, governor, carburetor, oil
pump, and many other parts starting at 1929 serial number 61059. These changes
included a smaller carburetor and an improved model of the Pierce governor.
    The 536-cubic inch Stearns engine was replaced by the 562.8-cubic inch
Allis-Chalmers engine starting at 1930 serial number 61698. The Stearns
Motor Manufacturing Company of Ludington, Michigan, was purchased by
Allis-Chalmers in that same year. This acquisition was probably made to obtain
the electrical generating equipment they built, as the Stearns engine design was
apparently discontinued.

Monarch Model 50 Standard Features
57-inch track gauge
Open cab
13-inch track shoes
Twin Disc clutch

Monarch Model 50 Hillside Special Standard Features
Open cab
Wide-track gauge version
15-, 18-, or 22-inch track shoes
Twin Disc clutch

Monarch Model 50 Blue Ox (logging) Standard Features
Has no cab

57-inch track gauge
13-inch cast grousers
Twin Disc clutch
Front and rear pull hooks
Grille, engine side, and crankcase shields

Production History (Monarch 50)

Year	Beginning number
1928	60298
1929	60611
1930	61559
1931	62147
Ending serial number	62297

Allis-Chalmers Monarch 75 Crawler (total production 1,066)

Nebraska test number (formerly Model F)	139
Serial numbers	70001–71066
Location of serial number	Front frame below radiator and on dash instruction plate
Production years	1928–1931
Total production	1,066
Engine	Beaver Le Roi four-cylinder vertical
Bore and stroke	
Engine numbers prior to 1353-1	6.50x7.0 inches
Engine number 1353-1 and up	6.75x7.0 inches
Rated rpm	850
Displacement	
Engine numbers prior to 1353-1	929 cubic inches
Engine number 1353-1 and up	1,002 cubic inches
Fuel	gasoline
Engine ratings	
Drawbar	78.17 horsepower
Belt	not tested
Maximum pull	20,050 pounds
Speed	
Standard 9-tooth chain drive sprockets	
First gear	1.55 mph
Second gear	2.64 mph
Third gear	3.56 mph
Reverse	2.64 mph
Optional 10-tooth chain drive sprockets	
First gear	1.72 mph
Second gear	2.93 mph
Third gear	3.96 mph
Reverse	2.93 mph

Descending from the original Monarch Model F-10 Ton, Allis-Chalmers sold the comparable Monarch 75 from 1928 to 1931. Using mainly riveted frame assemblies and chain-driven final drives; this crawler was not competitive with other makes of crawlers in its final years of production.

Optional 11-tooth chain drive sprockets	
First gear	1.89 mph
Second gear	3.23 mph
Third gear	4.35 mph
Reverse	3.23 mph
Optional 12-tooth chain drive sprockets	
First gear	2.07 mph
Second gear	3.52 mph
Third gear	4.75 mph
Reverse	3.52 mph
Length	158.69 inches
Standard track gauge	74 inches
Height (to top of radiator)	79.35 inches
Height (to top of cab)	104 inches
Weight	21,700 pounds
Carburetor	
Serial number 70001 to 70266	Zenith 77A
Serial number 70267 and up	Zenith 76
Ignition (magneto)	
Serial number 70001 to 70266	American Bosch ZR-4
Serial number 70267 and up	Eisemann GV-4

Air cleaner	
Serial number 70001 to 70039	United (twin type)
Serial number 70040 and up	Pomona
Standard track shoe width	16 inches
Number of shoes per track	33
Rollers per side	5
Fuel tank capacity	60 gallons
Cooling capacity	13 gallons
Crankcase oil capacity	28 quarts
Tune-up	
Spark plug used	7/8-inch
Spark plug gap	0.030 inches
Ignition point gap	0.015 inches
Price	$5,350 in 1929
Paint (1929 and later)	Persian Orange

Options

6.75-inch engine bore (standard feature at serial no. 70267)
16-inch regular, open, or smooth grousers (forged or manganese)
14.5-inch diameter by 11-inch wide pulley (420, 713, or 960 rpm)
PTO assembly (500, 850, or 1,150 rpm)
10-, 11-, or 12-tooth chain drive sprockets (9-tooth standard)
Special low-speed reverse gearing
Grille, headlight, and track shields
Two-man or three-man enclosed cab
Hydraulic system
Odometer (Ohmer type no. 76A)
Stewart-Warner vacuum tank
Rear hand starter (chain and sprocket) for models without electric starter
Auto-Lite ML4138 starter used with rear hand cranking device
Swivel drawbar
High-altitude pistons

Comments

The Monarch 75 was a newer version of the 10-ton Model F, which was built from 1926 to 1928. During these three years, 250 Model F units were built using the same engine, but with a Zenith L7T carburetor, American Bosch ZR4 magneto, and a United air cleaner. The undercarriage was somewhat different, but the Nebraska test for the 10-ton was used as the standard for the newer Model 75.

The Monarch 75 has a 48-link Baldwin chain from each final drive clutch assembly to the track drive sprocket assembly. Replacing the standard 9-tooth drive chain sprockets with 10-, 11-, or 12-tooth sprockets increases the crawler speeds.

Full-length truck sheds (angled track shields below the support rollers) were changed to partial type at 1929 serial number 70217 and up. At the same serial number, other changes occurred. A newer radiator had the Monarch name with larger lettering cast in the upper tank. The cylinder blocks and heads were strengthened, and the pistons had three compression rings instead of the previous two. The throttle control assembly was also changed.

Battery boxes were at the side of the motor until 1929 serial number 70232, when the batteries were dash-mounted.

At 1929 serial number 70267 and up, the engine was improved. Changes were made to the crankcase and cylinder block to accommodate changed engine accessories. A Le Roi brand governor replaced the Pierce MA-511 governor. The Zenith 76 replaced the Zenith 77A carburetor. The water pump was improved. The Eisemann GV-4 magneto replaced the American Bosch ZR-4. The 6.75-inch engine bore was optional prior to 1929 serial number 70267 and later became standard (engine number 1353-1 and after).

The transmission cover was changed at 1929 serial number 70317 and up. The newer cover provided the means of simultaneous steering clutch disengagement for operation of PTO attachments.

At 1929 serial number 70385 and up, the track used two upper track support rollers on each side instead of three, which were used on previous models.

Monarch 75 Standard Features
Open cab
16-inch grousers
Auto-Lite ML4137 starter plus lights
Rigid drawbar (redesigned at 1930 serial no. 70767 and up)

Monarch 75 Logger Standard Features
No cab
16-inch grousers
Auto-Lite ML4137 starter and lights (with headlight guards)
Crankcase, radiator, and track-release spring guard
Special 17.625-inch hand-starting crankshaft and guard
Special gearing (third and reverse)
Special high seat
Rigid drawbar and front pull hook

Production History (Monarch 75 models)

Year	Beginning number
1928	70001
1929	70208
1930	70655
1931	70895
Ending serial number	71066

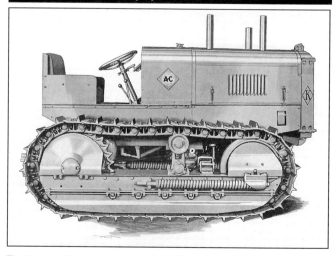

The Monarch 35 was renamed the Model K crawler in 1933. Two levers replaced the steering wheel when the transmission was upgraded from the original three-speed transmission to a four-speed in 1935 at serial number 4451. Production continued until 1943, when the HD-series crawlers overshadowed the Model K.

Allis-Chalmers Model 35, K, and KO Crawlers (three-speed) (total production 4,450)

Nebraska test number	215
Serial numbers (all K models)	1–9468
Serial numbers (three-speed models)	1–4450
Location of serial number and dash	top of transmission on right side
Location of engine number	left side of block
Production years (all K models)	1929–1943
Production years (three-speed models)	1929–1935
Total production (all K models)	approx. 8,300
Total production (three-speed models)	4,450
Engine	Allis-Chalmers vertical, four-cylinder I-head
Bore and stroke	
Serial numbers 1–2668	4.75x6.5 inches
Serial numbers 2669 and up	5.0x6.5 inches
Rated rpm	
Serial numbers 1–2668	930
Serial numbers 2669 and up	1,050

Displacement
    Serial numbers 1–2668 — 460 cubic inches
    Serial numbers 2669 and up — 510 cubic inches
Compression ratio
    Gasoline — 5.2:1
    Kerosene — 4.0:1
    Alcohol — 5.0:1
    Diesel — 6.5:1
Fuel
    Model K — gasoline, kerosene, or alcohol
    Model KO — diesel
Engine ratings (gasoline, 510 cubic inches)
    Drawbar — 47.87 horsepower
    PTO/belt — 55.24 horsepower
    Maximum pull — 8,865 pounds
Speed
    First gear — 2.08 mph
    Second gear — 3.1 mph
    Third gear — 4.5 mph
    Reverse — 2.39 mph
Length — 119.56 inches
Standard track gauge — 48 inches
Height (to top tank of radiator)
    Model K — 64 inches
    Model KO — 61.5 inches
Weight
    Model K — 11,670 pounds
    Model KO — 11,870 pounds
Carburetor (nondiesel models)
    Serial numbers 1–50 — Kingston M
    Serial number 51 to engine
        no. 13166 — Zenith C6EV
Diesel injector pump — Bosch
Ignition
    Nondiesel models (magneto)
    Serial numbers 1–3126 (approx.) — Eisemann GL-4
    Serial numbers 3127 (approx.)
        to 4671 — Bendix-Scintilla C-4
    Diesel magneto — Mallory
Air cleaner
    Serial numbers 1–50 — Allis-Chalmers
    Serial numbers 51 and up — Vortox
Standard track shoe width
    Serial numbers 1–2668 — 13 inches
    Serial 2669 and up — 15 inches
Number shoes per track — 34
Rollers per side — 5
Fuel tank capacity — 34 gallons
Cooling capacity — 10 gallons
Crankcase oil capacity
    Model K — 14 quarts
    Model KO — 16 quarts

Transmission oil capacity	5.5 gallons
Final drive oil capacity (each)	5 quarts
Tune-up (Model K)	
Firing order	1-3-4-2
Spark plug used	Champion W-10
Spark plug gap	0.025 inches
Ignition point gap	0.015 inches (Eisemann)
Timing	26 degrees BTDC (flywheel)
Price	
Model K (gasoline)	$2,400 in 1934
Model KO (diesel)	$3,150 in 1934
Model WK (wide)	$2,545 in 1934
Paint	Persian Orange

Options

WK (wide) 63-inch track gauge instead of the standard 48 inches
Track shoe widths of 7, 13, and 15 inches (Model K and KO)
Track shoes widths of 7 to 28 inches (Model WK and WKO)
Track shoe styles of standard, smooth, open, and rubber-faced
Track shoe styles of skeleton, ice and snow, angle iron, dirt, or street
Kerosene burning equipment
Special gearing: lower first, lower reverse, or higher third gear
Winter cab or canopy (curtains optional)
Track fenders
Radiator and crankcase guards
Front bumper and pull hook
Engine covers
Muffler or spark arrester
Odometer (transmission case type)
Side seat arrangement
PTO assembly: engine speed, reduction (527 rpm), or double
10- or 12-inch diameter by 8.75-inch wide power pulley (1,050 rpm)
12-volt Auto-Lite MAH-4003 starter (prior to serial no. 51)
12-volt Auto-Lite ML-4123 or ML-4177 starter (serial no. 51 and up)
Lights (guards offered)
Rear handcrank starting assembly
Painting other than standard

Comments

The Model K was the new name that Allis-Chalmers gave to the Monarch 35 model in 1933, five years after the company purchased Monarch Tractor Inc.

Serial numbers 1 to 50 had an engine block and crankshaft with 2.5-inch main bearings instead of the 3.0-inch bearings found on later models. While later K tractors had a V-fan belt and pulleys, these 50 models had a flat fan belt and pulleys.

The 1929 to 1930 serial numbers, 1 to 50, had Allis-Chalmers air cleaners mounted at the rear of the engines. The 1930 and 1931 serial numbers, 51 to 1479, had Vortox air cleaners mounted at the rear of the engines. The 1931 to 1943 serial numbers, 1480 and up, had Vortox air cleaners mounted at the front of the engines.

The drawbars on K models prior to 1930 serial number 1306 had a pair of rod braces for support. The 1930 to 1933 serial numbers, 1306 to 2668, had triangular plate braces on the drawbar. The 1933 to 1935 serial numbers, 2669 to 3700, had plate braces and a cast steel drawbar instead of the flat steel type on other units. The 1935 to 1943 serial numbers, 3701 and up, had plate-steel braces and an improved stirrup pivot to replace a single bolt for the drawbar.

Prior to 1931 serial number 1901, the 12-volt battery was under the seat. Serial numbers 1901 to 4450 had the battery box at the side of the seat. The 1935 to 1936 serial numbers, 4451 to 6268, had the battery under the seat. All serial numbers after that had a pair of 6-volt batteries under the seat.

The undercarriage was redesigned for strength with the 1933 serial number 2669 and up.

Serial numbers 3119 to 5450, from 1934 to 1936, had a heat gauge on the water manifold.

The diesel engine version, Model K-O, was available in 1934. This model was very similar to the regular model with the exception of the spark ignition diesel engine and related accessories.

At 1935 serial number 4451 and up, two levers replaced the steering wheel and the transmission was changed to a four-speed.

Model K and K-O (three-speed) Standard Features
48-inch track gauge (7-foot turning radius)
Upholstered seat
Three-speed transmission
Steering wheel (operates final drive clutches)
Complete set of tools and grease gun

Model WK (three-speed) Standard Features
63-inch track gauge (8-foot turning radius)
Upholstered seat
Three-speed transmission
Steering wheel (operates final drive clutches)
Complete set of tools and grease gun

Production History (all K models)

Year	Beginning number
1929	1
1930	49
1931	1373
1932	2334
1933	2654
1934	3046 and KO5200
1935	3594
1936	4793 and KO6019
1937	6336
1938	7708
1939	8018
1940	8523
1941	8957
1942	9269
1943	9394
Ending serial number	9468

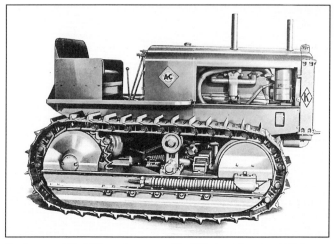

The four-speed Model K crawler came out in 1935 at serial number 4451. As one of the first four-speed crawlers on the market, sales of this model were good. Steering levers replaced the steering wheel of previous models, making the newer crawler even more modern.

Allis-Chalmers Model K and KO Crawlers (four-speed) (total production approx. 3,850)

Nebraska test numbers	285 and 336
Serial numbers (all K models)	1–9468
Serial numbers (four-speed models)	4451 to 9468
Location of serial number	rear side of transmission at top right and dash
Location of engine number	left side of block at lower center
Production years (all K models)	1929–1943
Production years (four-speed models)	1935–1943
Total production (all K models)	approx. 8,300
Total production (four-speed models)	approx. 3,850
Engine	Allis-Chalmers vertical, four-cylinder I-head
Bore and stroke	5.0x6.5 inches
Rated rpm	1,050
Displacement	510 cubic inches
Compression ratio	
Gasoline	5.2:1
Kerosene	4.0:1
Alcohol	5.0:1

Butane	5.8:1
Diesel	6.5:1
Fuel	
Model K	gasoline, kerosene, alcohol, or butane
Model KO	diesel
Engine ratings (wide track models tested)	
Gasoline (test number 336)	
Drawbar	53.60 horsepower
PTO/belt	62.22 horsepower
Maximum pull	11,785 pounds
Diesel (test number 285)	
Drawbar	49.26 horsepower
PTO/belt	59.06 horsepower
Maximum pull	11,685 pounds
Speed	
First gear	1.72 mph
Second gear	2.59 mph
Third gear	3.26 mph
Fourth gear	5.92 mph
Reverse	2.10 mph
Length	119.56 inches
Standard track gauge	48 inches
Height (to top tank of radiator)	
Model K	64 inches
Model KO	61.5 inches
Weight (WK)	13,340 pounds
Carburetor	
Serial number 51 to engine number 13165	Zenith C6EV
Engine number 13166 and up	Zenith AM-41207
Diesel injector pump	Bosch
Ignition	
Nondiesel models (magneto)	
Serial numbers 3127 to 4671	Bendix-Scintilla C4
Serial numbers 4672 and up	Fairbanks-Morse FM4B
Diesel (magneto)	Mallory
Air cleaner	Vortox
Standard track shoe width	15 inches
Number of shoes per track	34
Rollers per side	5
Fuel tank capacity	39 gallons
Cooling capacity	11.5 gallons
Crankcase oil capacity	
Model K	14 quarts
Model KO	16 quarts
Transmission oil capacity	5.5 gallons
Final drive oil capacity (each)	5 quarts
Tune-up	
Firing order	1-3-4-2
Spark plug used (gasoline)	Champion W-10

Spark plug used (diesel fuel)	Champion W-95D
Spark plug gap	
Nondiesel fuel models	0.025–0.030 inches
Diesel fuel models	0.020–0.025 inches
Ignition point gap	0.020 inches (Fairbanks)
Timing	26 degrees BTDC
Price	
Model K	$2,835 in 1943
Model WK	$3,024 in 1943
Paint	Persian Orange

Options
Wide, 63-inch track gauge (WK and WKO)
Diesel oil versions (KO and WKO)
Kerosene burning equipment
Track shoe widths of 7, 13, and 15 inches (Model K and KO)
Track shoe widths of 7 to 28 inches (Model WK and WKO)
Track shoe styles of standard, smooth, open, and rubber-faced
Track shoe styles of skeleton, ice and snow, angle iron, dirt, or street
Radiator guard (light or heavy-duty)
Crankcase guards and engine covers
Front bumper and pull hook
Engine speed PTO assembly, regular or reversible
Reduction-type PTO assembly (595 rpm)
10- or 12-inch diameter by 8.75-inch wide power pulley (1,050 rpm)
Canopy (curtains available)
12-volt Auto-Lite ML-4123 or ML-4177 starter
12-volt lights (guards offered)
Rear starting crank assembly

Comments
Crawlers with serial numbers prior to 4672 (approximately) had a governor assembly with a base-mount magneto. On later models, the assembly was designed for a flange-mount magneto.
The 1936 serial number 6269 and up had pinion and bull gears with improved teeth.

Model K and K-O (four-speed) Standard Features
48-inch track gauge (7-foot turning radius)
15-inch standard grousers
Upholstered seat
Four-speed sliding-gear transmission
Track fenders (optional on three-speed models)

Model WK and WKO (four-speed) Standard Features
63-inch track gauge (8-foot turning radius)
15-inch standard grousers
Upholstered seat
Four-speed sliding-gear transmission
Track fenders (optional on three-speed models)

Allis-Chalmers Model L and LO Crawlers (steering wheel) (total production 1,162, excluding LO Models)

Nebraska test number	200
Serial numbers (all L models)	1–3357
Serial numbers (steering wheel models)	1–1162
Location of serial number	shelf at right side of rear end of transmission case
Location of engine number	right side of block at lower center
Production years (all L models)	1931–1942
Production years (steering wheel models)	1931–1935
Total production (all L models)	3,357
Total production (steering wheel models)	1,162
Engine	Allis-Chalmers vertical, six-cylinder I-head
Bore and stroke	5.25x6.5 inches
Rated rpm	1,050
Displacement	844 cubic inches
Compression ratio	4.4:1 (gasoline)
Fuel	gasoline or diesel
Engine ratings (gasoline)	
Drawbar	76.01 horsepower
PTO/belt	91.93 horsepower
Maximum pull	15,086 pounds
Speed	
First gear	1.94 mph
Second gear	2.45 mph
Third gear	3.05 mph
Fourth gear	4.1 mph
Fifth gear	5.2 mph
Sixth gear	6.47 mph
Reverse	1.45 and 3.07 mph
Length	153.25 inches
Standard track gauge	68 inches
Height (to top tank of radiator)	81 inches
Weight	
Model L	22,027 pounds
Model LO	23,100 pounds
Carburetor (two used)	Zenith 6EV
Ignition (magneto)	Eisemann GV6
Air cleaner	
Serial numbers prior to 26	Vortox 930
Serial number 26 and up	Vortox 2300D
Standard grouser width	16 inches
Number of shoes per track	35
Rollers per side	5
Fuel tank capacity	75 gallons

Cooling capacity	19 gallons
Crankcase oil capacity	
Model L	24 quarts
Model LO	26 quarts
Transmission oil capacity	10 gallons
Final drive oil capacity (each)	8 quarts
Tune-up	
Firing order	1-4-2-6-3-5
Spark plug used (gasoline)	Champion W-14
Spark plug gap	0.030 inches
Ignition point gap	0.015 inches
Price	
Gasoline (L)	$4,650 in 1934
Diesel (LO)	$5,950 in 1934
Paint	Persian Orange

Options

Lower-speed transmission gears
12-volt Auto-Lite ML4123, ML4177, or EO5129 starter
Lights (guards available)
Auxiliary 60-gallon fuel tank
18- or 20-inch diameter by 15-inch wide pulley (444 and 580 rpm)
Canopy (curtains available) or enclosed winter cab
Odometer
Rear starting crank
Muffler or spark arrester (two used)
Full cushioned back seat
Radiator curtain
Hood side plates
Front bumper and pull hook
Narrow or full crankcase guard
16-, 20-, and 24-inch grousers
Track shoe styles of skeleton, smooth, open, and smooth open
Ice, dirt and snow, or angle iron grousers or street plates

Comments

    At 1931 serial number 26, the water pump, track rollers, and front idler had improved bearings. The first 25 crawlers had several different gears in the transmission.

    Beginning at 1934 serial number 678, the 1.5-inch wide frame rails were replaced by 2-inch frame rails.

    The throttle lever was changed from a ratchet to a friction-disc type at 1934 serial number 699 and up.

    Model LO (spark ignition diesel) was introduced in 1934 with its own serial numbers. Production figures for later years have not been found by this author.

Model L Crawler Standard Features

16-inch grousers
68-inch track gauge (9-foot turning radius)
Set of tools with a large and small grease gun

Model L and LO Crawlers (steering levers)

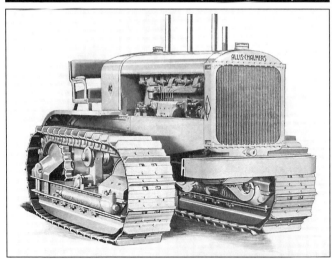

Two levers replaced the steering wheel on the Model L crawler in 1935 at serial number 1163. The optional oil engine Model LO used diesel fuel, but fired it with spark plugs instead of using high engine compression as on true diesels.

Production History (all L crawlers)

Year	Beginning number
1931	1
1932	35
1933	499
1934	661 and LO1547
1935	888
1936	1439
1937	2137
1938	2706
1939	2944
1940	3233
1941	3252
1942	3273
Ending serial number	3357

Allis-Chalmers Model L and LO Crawlers (steering levers) (total production 2,195, excluding LO models)

Nebraska test numbers	287 and 338
Serial numbers (all L models)	1–3357
Serial numbers (steering lever models)	1163–3357

Location of serial number	shelf on right side at rear end of transmission case
Location of engine number	right side of block at lower center
Production years (all L models)	1931–1942
Production years (steering lever models)	1935–1942
Total production (all L models)	3,357
Total production (steering lever models)	2,195
Engine	Allis-Chalmers vertical, six-cylinder I-head
Bore and stroke	5.25x6.5 inches
Rated rpm	1,050
Displacement	844 cubic inches
Compression ratio	
Gasoline (prior to engine number 3518)	4.4:1
Gasoline (engine number 3518 and up)	5.2:1
Diesel (Model LO)	6.5:1
Engine ratings	
Gasoline (test number 338, for engine numbers 3518 and up)	
Drawbar	91.99 horsepower
PTO/belt	108.84 horsepower
Maximum pull	23,851 pounds
Diesel (test number 287)	
Drawbar	76.75 horsepower
PTO/belt	91.56 horsepower
Maximum pull	20,273 pounds
Speed	
First gear	1.48 mph
Second gear	1.94 mph
Third gear	2.68 mph
Fourth gear	3.50 mph
Fifth gear	4.90 mph
Sixth gear	6.41 mph
Reverse (low)	1.72 mph
Reverse (high)	2.25 mph
Length	153.25 inches
Standard track gauge	68 inches
Height (to top tank of radiator)	81 inches
Weight (gasoline)	26,105 pounds
Carburetor (two used)	
Engine number prior to 3518	Zenith C6EV
Engine numbers 3518 and up	Zenith 62AXJ10
Ignition	
Gasoline (magneto)	
Prior to engine number 1718	Eisemann GV-6 or Fairbanks-Morse RV6B
Engine numbers 1718–2485	Bendix C6
Serial numbers 1432–1875	Fairbanks-Morse RV6

Serial number 1876 to engine no. 3687	Fairbanks-Morse RV6B
Engine numbers 3688 and up	Fairbanks-Morse FM-06B
Diesel (distributor)	Mallory MO-4
Air cleaner	
Gasoline	Vortox
Diesel	United
Standard grouser width	
Model L (prior to June 10, 1937)	16 inches
Model L (after June 10, 1937)	20 inches
Model LO	20 inches
Number of shoes per track	35
Rollers per side	5
Fuel tank capacity	75 gallons
Cooling capacity	19 gallons
Crankcase oil capacity	
Model L	24 quarts
Model LO	26 quarts
Transmission oil capacity	10 gallons
Final drive oil capacity (each)	8 quarts
Tune-up	
Firing order	1-4-2-6-3-5
Spark plug used	
Gasoline	Champion W-14
Diesel fuel	Champion W-95D
Spark plug gap	
Gasoline	0.030 inches
Diesel fuel	0.022 inches
Ignition point gap (Fairbanks and Mallory)	0.020 inches
Timing	
Diesel (injection)	60 degrees BTDC
Price	
Gasoline	$5,302 in 1942
Diesel	$6,600 in 1942
Paint	Persian Orange

Options
Track shoe widths of 14, 16, 20, and 24 inches
Track shoe styles of standard, smooth, open, and skeleton
Track shoe styles of ice, dirt and snow, angle iron, or street
12-volt Auto-Lite ML-4123 or EO-5129 starter
12-volt battery lighting
6-volt nonbattery lighting (Bosch ARJF 75/6-900 A14 generator)
Auxiliary 60-gallon fuel tank
18- or 20-inch diameter by 15-inch wide pulley (444 and 580 rpm)
Canopy (curtains available) or enclosed winter cab
Odometer (Stewart-Warner 76-D)
Rear starting crank
Spark arrester, regular muffler, or heavy-duty muffler (two used)
Full-cushioned back seat

Special seat frame (4 inches higher)
Radiator curtain
Hood side plates
Front bumper and pull hook (standard on LO)
Narrow or full crankcase guard
Light- or heavy-duty radiator guard

Comments

At serial number 1366 and up, the gearing in the transmission was changed and the speeds were reduced slightly.

An engine air precleaner was used at 1936 serial number 1881 and up.

The cast drawbar arm was replaced by a flat steel arm at 1937 serial number 2360 and up.

At 1939 serial number 3031 and up, the steering levers were made heavier.

Steering clutches were improved for longer life at the 1940 serial number 3273 and up.

When the compression ratio and corresponding horsepower was increased at engine number 3518, the valves were made heavier, the carburetor model was changed, and the three-valve cover breather caps were reduced to one.

In 1939, Allis-Chalmers made 10 Model LD crawlers, serial numbers 8 to 17. These experimental crawlers were General Motors diesel-injected engine models.

Model L Crawler Standard Features
20-inch grousers
68-inch track gauge (9-foot turning radius)
Set of tools with a large and small grease gun

Model LO Crawler Standard Features
20-inch grousers
68-inch track gauge (9-foot turning radius)
Front bumper and pull hook
Set of tools with a large and small grease gun

Model LL Logger Standard Features
Grille and rear seat guards
Front bumper and pull hook
Extra side and bottom and track guards
Special transmission gearing

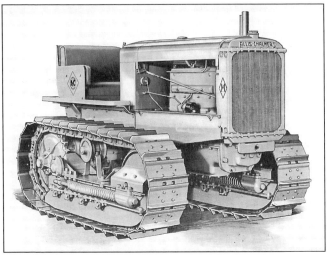

Using the same Allis-Chalmers engine as the Model U tractor, this Model M crawler was introduced in 1932 and sold more than 14,500 copies before production ended in 1942. This machine was about half the Model K in horsepower and weight.

Allis-Chalmers Model M Crawler (total production 14,524)

Nebraska test numbers	216 and 239
Serial numbers	1–14524
Location of serial number	right side of transmission case, by clutch inspection cover
Location of engine number	right side of block under oil fill elbow
Production years	1932–1942
Total production	14,524
Engine	Allis-Chalmers vertical, four-cylinder I-head
Bore and stroke	
Prior to serial number 2942	4.375x5 inches
Serial number 2942 and up	4.50x5 inches
Rated rpm	1,200
Displacement	
Prior to serial number 2942	300 cubic inches
Serial number 2942 and up	318 cubic inches
Compression ratio	
Gasoline	4.75:1
Distillate	4.2:1

Fuel	gasoline or distillate
Engine ratings (300 cubic inches)	
Gasoline (test number 216)	
Drawbar	29.65 horsepower
PTO/belt	35.43 horsepower
Maximum pull	5,166 pounds
Distillate (test number 239)	
Drawbar	28.66 horsepower
PTO/belt	35.05 horsepower
Maximum pull	5,576 pounds
Speed	
First gear	1.83 mph
Second gear	2.23 mph
Third gear	3.20 mph
Fourth gear	4.15 mph
Reverse	2.55 mph
Length	101.375 inches
Standard track gauge	40 inches
Height (to top tank of radiator)	56.19 inches
Weight (gasoline)	6,620 pounds
Carburetor	Zenith K5
Ignition (magneto)	Eisemann GL4, Bendix C-4, or Fairbanks-Morse FMK4B
Air cleaner	Vortox or Donaldson
Standard track shoe width	12 inches
Number of shoes per track	31
Rollers per side	4
Fuel tank capacity	24 gallons
Cooling capacity	6 gallons
Crankcase oil capacity	10 quarts
Transmission oil capacity	3 gallons
Final drive oil capacity (each)	5 quarts
Tune-up	
Firing order	1-2-4-3
Spark plug used (gasoline)	Champion W-14
Spark plug gap	0.035 inches
Ignition point gap	0.020 inches (Fairbanks)
Timing	32 degrees BTDC (flywheel)
Price (gasoline)	
Model M	$1,650 in 1934
Model M	$1,780 in 1942
Paint	Persian Orange

Options

Track shoe widths of 7 and 12 inches (standard M crawler)
Track shoe widths of 7, 12, 14, 16, 18, and 22 inches (Model WM)
Track shoe styles of standard, open, rubber-faced, and angle iron
Side-mount seat and controls for special road work
Canopy top (optional curtains available)
Winter cab (full glass enclosure) or canopy

Alcohol changeover group
Odometer
Light or heavy radiator guards
6-volt Auto-Lite MAB-046 starter with lights
Nonbattery lighting (KW model T6 or Bosch RJF 75/6 generator)
PTO assembly: engine speed or gear reduction (536 rpm)
10- or 12-inch diameter by 8.75-inch wide belt pulley (960 rpm)
10- or 12-inch diameter by 7.75-inch wide belt pulley for Orchard model with
    top seat
Engine covers and crankcase guard
Track fenders
Front pull hook
Painting other than standard

Comments

At 1936 serial number 2942 and up, the Model M crawler had the engine bore increased from 3.375 inches to 3.50 inches. This crawler used the same engine as the popular Model U farm tractor.

In 1938 at serial number 7742 and up, the starting fuel tank was moved from the front to the rear of the main fuel tank.

The steering clutch levers were improved at 1939 serial number 8196 and up.

In 1939 at serial number 8342 and up, the front track idler and track rollers were changed from a bushing design to a tapered roller bearing design.

The transmission oil fill neck was on the rear transmission cover until 1939. Beginning with serial number 8386, the oil fill was relocated at the oil gauge rod assembly in the front of the transmission top cover.

Allis-Chalmers Model M serial number 1 resides in a museum at Vista, California.

Model M Standard Features
40-inch track gauge (72-inch turning radius)
Seven-leaf front equalizing spring
31-link track chain with 12-inch grousers
Hand-operated master clutch

Model WM (Hillside Special) Standard Features
50-inch track gauge (78-inch turning radius)
12-inch grousers
Rigid track frame
35-link track chain prior to serial number 7710
37-link track chain on models built at serial number 7710 and up
Foot-operated master clutch

Model M Logger Standard Features
Engine and crankcase shields
Grille and sprocket guards
31-link track chain

Model M Orchard Standard Features
Full-length track fenders and engine side shields (louvered)
Grille guard
Seat located rear of tracks or low on top

Operator controls extended back on model with seat behind tracks
31-link track chain

Production History (Model M crawlers)

Year	Beginning number
1932	1
1933	42
1934	402
1935	842
1936	1942
1937	3842
1938	7067
1939	8127
1940	9540
1941	11380
1942	12947
Ending serial number	14524

Allis-Chalmers Model S and SO Crawlers (total production 1,225)

Nebraska test numbers	286 and 337
Serial numbers	3–1227
Location of serial number	rear of transmission case on upper right and dash
Location of engine number	plate on left side of block at lower center
Production years	1937–1942
Total production (all S models)	1,225
Engine (all S models)	Allis-Chalmers vertical, four-cylinder I-head
Bore and stroke (all S models)	5.75x6.50 inches
Rated rpm (all S models)	1,050
Displacement (all S models)	675.1 cubic inches
Compression ratio	
Gasoline	5.0:1
Diesel (SO model)	6.5:1
Fuel	gasoline or diesel fuel
Engine ratings	
Gasoline (test no. 337)	
Drawbar	68.86 horsepower
PTO/belt	84.34 horsepower
Maximum pull	17,843 pounds
Diesel fuel (test no. 286)	
Drawbar	62.39 horsepower
PTO/belt	74.82 horsepower
Maximum pull	16,732 pounds
Speed	
First gear	1.52 mph
Second gear	2.32 mph

Third gear	3.25 mph
Fourth gear	4.55 mph
Fifth gear	6.37 mph
Reverse	1.76 mph
Length	146 inches
Standard track gauge	62 inches
Height	74 inches
Weight (shipping)	
Model S	18,970 pounds
Model WS	19,490 pounds
Carburetor	Zenith 62AJ-12
Diesel injection pump	Deco
Ignition (distributor)	
Gasoline	Delco-Remy 1111510
Diesel fuel	Mallory MO4
Air cleaner	United
Standard track shoe width	18 inches
Number of shoes per track	32
Rollers per side	5
Fuel tank capacity	64 gallons
Cooling capacity	12.5 gallons
Crankcase oil capacity	20 quarts
Transmission oil capacity	5.75 gallons
Final drive oil capacity (each)	8 quarts
Tune-up	
Firing order	1-3-4-2
Spark plug used	
Gasoline (pre-1942 models)	Champion W-14
Gasoline (1942)	Champion J-8
Diesel	Champion W-95D
Spark plug gap	0.025 inches
Ignition point gap	0.020 inches
Timing	
Diesel fuel	60 degrees BTDC
Price (Model S)	$4,095 in 1942

Options

Track shoe widths of 16, 18, 20, 22, and 24 inches
Track shoe styles of standard, smooth, open, and rubber-faced
13.375-inch diameter by 10-inch wide power pulley (770 rpm)
PTO assembly (2.75-inch tapered, 283–337 rpm)
Louvered engine covers
High-altitude pistons
Ignition switch lock (serial number 1149 and up)

Comments

A Purolator oil filter assembly was used on engine numbers 1 to 6 and 52 and up. Other engines had a Michiana oil filter assembly.

Fuel tanks prior to 1939 serial number 605 have a float and dial-type fuel gauge. All afterwards have a fuel gauge rod.

Positive-seal track rollers with tapered bearings replaced composition-seal rollers with straight roller bearings at 1939 serial number 628 and up. Positive-seal front track idlers with tapered bearings replaced composition seal front idlers with straight bearings at 1939 serial number 703 and up.

A 36-inch exhaust pipe replaced an 18-inch pipe at 1939 serial number 1069 and up. Crawlers from serial numbers 736 to 1068 used a flared exhaust pipe extension with an angle-cut top.

The master clutch was redesigned at 1941 serial number 1199 and up. The newer clutch used the same plate, but had a sturdier release bearing assembly.

Model S Standard Features
62-inch track gauge (99-inch turning radius)
15.5-inch ground clearance
18-inch grousers (maximum width)
12-volt Auto-Lite EO-5129 starter
Upholstered seat
Drawbar (32-inch lateral adjustment)
Five-speed constant-mesh transmission

Model WS and WSO (wide) Standard Features
74-inch track gauge (108-inch turning radius)
15.5-inch ground clearance
18-inch grousers
12-volt Auto-Lite EO-5129 starter
Upholstered seat
Drawbar (32-inch lateral adjustment)
Five-speed constant-mesh transmission

Production History (all S crawler models)

Year	Beginning number
1937	3
1938	413
1939	585
1940	1085
1941	1128
1942	1212
Ending serial number	1227

Allis-Chalmers Model HD-14 and HD-14C Crawlers (total production 6,405)

Nebraska test number	362
Serial numbers	18–6422
Location of serial number	top of flange on right rear side of transmission case
Location of engine number	right side of block by governor
Production years	1939–1947
Total production	6,405
Engine	General Motors vertical, six-cylinder diesel (two-cycle)
Bore and stroke	4.25x5.0 inches
Rated rpm	
HD14 model	1,500
HD14C model	1,650
Displacement	425 cubic inches
Compression ratio	16.0:1
Fuel	diesel
Engine ratings (HD14)	
Drawbar	126.98 horsepower
PTO/belt	145.39 horsepower
Maximum pull	28,018 pounds
Speed (HD14 model)	
First gear	1.72 mph
Second gear	2.18 mph
Third gear	2.76 mph
Fourth gear	3.50 mph
Fifth gear	4.36 mph
Sixth gear	7.00 mph
Reverse (low)	2.00 mph
Reverse (high)	3.20 mph
Speed (HD14C model)	
First range	0–3.1 mph
Second range	0–3.8 mph
Third range	0–7.2 mph
Reverse	0–3.5 mph
Length	165 inches
Standard track gauge	68 inches
Height	108.75 inches
Weight	
HD14 model	28,750 pounds
HD14C model	29,330 pounds
Injector (plunger type)	GM unit injector 6-006-155 or 6-006-155-0
Air cleaner	United (two units)
Standard track shoe width	22 inches
Number of shoes per track	35
Rollers per side	5
Fuel tank capacity	68 gallons
Cooling capacity	12 gallons
Crankcase oil capacity	14 quarts

Transmission oil capacity (HD-14)	10 gallons
Final drive oil capacity (each)	8 quarts
Tune-up	
Firing order	1-5-3-6-2-4
Injector timing (special tool used)	1.484 inches, plunger follower to injector body, valves open
Price	$9,250 in 1947
Paint	

Crawler is painted Persian Orange, yellow, or olive drab (military)

Options
Various grouser styles and widths up to 24 inches
Engine preheater
Cab or canopy (curtains available)
PTO assembly (935 rpm)
20-inch diameter by 15-inch wide belt pulley (405 or 650 rpm)
20-inch diameter by 15-inch wide belt pulley (585 rpm on HD-14C)

Comments
The HD-14 model had a manual transmission that was improved at 1941 serial number 759. The spline and size of the pinion shaft was changed and two bearings were changed from ball to roller-type. Four gears were changed from 20-degree pressure angle teeth to 25-degree pressure angle.

The HD-14C model had a torque converter transmission and was introduced in 1946.

Steering clutches were improved, effective with 1942 serial number 2079. The newer units were ventilated and adjustable for longer clutch life.

Model HD-14 Standard Features
22-inch grousers
Front bumper
Odometer
Skeleton sprocket

Production History (HD-14 and HD-14C models)

Year	Beginning number
1939	18
1940	26
1941	549
1942	1166
1943	2113
1944	3138
1945	4259
1946	5455
1947	5815
Ending serial number	6422

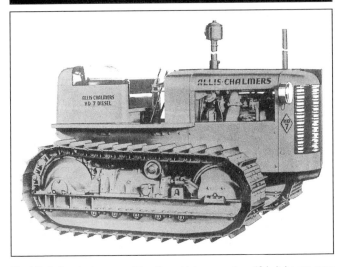

The HD-7 Crawler became a big seller with its more than 68 belt horsepower and efficient General Motors diesel engine. The reliability of this machine was reinforced by the fact that the military used many of them during World War II.

Allis-Chalmers Model HD-7 Crawler (total production 18,503)

Nebraska test number	360
Serial numbers	3–18505
Location of serial number	back of transmission case at upper right corner
Location of engine number	right side of block by governor
Production years	1940–1950
Total production	18,503
Engine	General Motors vertical, three-cylinder diesel (two-cycle)
Bore and stroke	4.25x5.0 inches
Rated rpm	1,500
Displacement	213 cubic inches
Compression ratio	16.0:1
Fuel	diesel
Engine ratings (HD7W)	
Drawbar	57.29 horsepower
PTO/belt	68.68 horsepower
Maximum pull	12,171 pounds
Speed	
First gear	1.59 mph
Second gear	2.19 mph
Third gear	2.97 mph

Fourth gear	5.00 mph
Reverse	1.89 mph
Length (standard 34-shoe track)	128 inches
Standard track gauge	63 inches
Height	86 inches
Weight	
HD7 model	13,835 pounds
HD7W model	14,175 pounds
Injector (plunger type)	GM unit injector 6-006-155 or 6-006-155-0
Air cleaner	United
Standard track shoe width	16 inches
Number of shoes per track	
Standard model	34
Special	36
Long track	38
Rollers per side	
Standard	5
Long track	6
Fuel tank capacity	31 gallons
Cooling capacity	5.75 gallons
Crankcase oil capacity	11 quarts
Transmission oil capacity	
Prior to 1947	5.25 gallons
1947 and later	6.5 gallons
Final drive oil capacity (each)	
Prior to 1947	4 quarts
1947 and later	7 quarts
Tune-up	
Firing order	1-3-2
Injector timing (special tool used)	1.484 inches, plunger follower to injector body, valves open
Price	
Model HD-7	$6,900 in 1950
Model HD-7W	$6,980 in 1950
Paint	Persian Orange, yellow and olive drab (military)

Options

PTO assembly: straight (889 rpm) or reduction (574 rpm)
PTO assembly (reversible reduction)
10- or 12-inch diameter by 8.75-inch wide power pulley assembly
Canopy top (curtains available)
Three-man cab (windshield opens, precleaner relocated by a duct)
Front bumper and front hook
Odometer (miles or kilometers)
Cold weather starting aid
Grouser widths of 7, 13, 15, and 16 inches (HD-7)
Grousers widths of 7 to 26 inches (HD-7W)
Larger track idler (standard on post-1945 long-track models)
11-inch, rubber-faced track shoes

Hot-climate radiator (four rows of cores instead of three)
Reverse-flow radiator fan
Radiator screen (to avoid clogging by leaves and such)
Air precleaner extension and tripod bracing
Engine side guards and brake lever guards (for logging)

Comments

Agricultural models had a front stabilizer spring-mounted track frame, while industrial models had a rigid-beam front support.

The fuel system was improved with a more effective sump and filter system at 1940 serial number 303 and up.

The radiator was improved from six fins per inch to seven per inch at 1940 serial number 323. The 2-inch-deep radiator fan was changed to 2.5 inches at 1940 serial number 482. The fan was changed again to 3 inches at 1947 serial number 13453.

Three different types of air precleaners were used on the HD-7 crawlers. The first type, used until 1940 serial number 403, had a dust jar and was mounted below the hood and attached to the top casting of the main air cleaner. The second type was used from serial number 403 to approximately 788 and was a stack-mounted type with a removable dust jar. The final type was stack-mounted with a sight glass in the dome-shaped metal shell.

Longer track versions of 36- and 38-shoe tracks became available after 1940 serial number 1102. At the same time, seals in the track components of all HD-7 crawlers were improved.

During World War II, apparently about 5,000 HD-7W military crawlers, referred to as the Medium Tractor M1, were built. It appears that during 1944 and 1945, only wide-track versions were built; probably most were for the military.

The front idler on the long-track model was increased from a 23.5-inch diameter to a 27.5-inch diameter standard feature at 1945 serial number 11497.

The final drive assemblies were changed with the 40-tooth drive gear and 9-tooth pinion being replaced by a 49-tooth drive gear and 11-tooth pinion at 1946 serial number 12858.

The starting aid for HD-7 crawlers built before 1948 serial number 16697 was an air heater that uses fuel oil pumped by hand and fired at a nozzle to preheat intake air. At serial number 16697 and up, the standard starting aid was an ether capsule dispenser mounted on the right side of the cowl.

Model HD-7 Standard Features

52-inch track gauge
16-inch grousers
12-volt Delco-Remy 1108714 starter plus lights
6-volt batteries (2)
Muffler
Crankcase and track guards
Radiator shutter

Model HD-7W (wide) Standard Features

63-inch track gauge
16-inch grousers
12-volt Delco-Remy 1108714 starter plus lights

6-volt batteries (two)
Muffler
Crankcase and track guards
Radiator shutter

Production History (HD-7 models, 52-inch track gauge)*

Year	Beginning number
1940	3
1941	503
1942	1137
1943	5403
1944	not found
1945	not found
1946	12382
1947	13236
1948	15117
1949	16769
1950	18094

Ending serial number (all HD-7 models)   18505
*The starting serial numbers for the HD-7W are not the same as the standard model, although the two lists are interspersed with each other.

Production History (HD-7W models, 63-inch track gauge)

Year	Beginning number
1940	3
1941	503
1942	1137
1943	2977W
1944	5285W
1945	7998W
1946	12091W
1947	13078W
1948	15156W
1949	16752W
1950	18086W

The 10-ton Model HD-10 sold rather well compared to the Model SO crawler that it was built to replace. The four-cylinder General Motors diesel engine gave this machine more than 98 belt horsepower.

Allis-Chalmers Model HD-10 Crawler (total production 10,197)

Nebraska test number	361
Serial numbers	2–10,198
Location of serial numbers	back of transmission case at upper right corner
Location of engine number	right side of block by governor
Production years	1940–1950
Total production	10,197
Engine	General Motors vertical, four-cylinder diesel (two-cycle)
Bore and stroke	4.25x5.0 inches
Rated rpm	1,600
Displacement	284 cubic inches
Compression ratio	16.0:1
Fuel	diesel
Engine ratings	
Drawbar	82.19 horsepower
PTO/belt	98.47 horsepower
Maximum pull	19,002 pounds
Speed	
First gear	1.49 mph
Second gear	2.39 mph
Third gear	3.37 mph
Fourth gear	3.91 mph

Fifth gear	5.38 mph
Sixth gear	8.81 mph
Reverse (low)	1.65 mph
Reverse (high)	3.71 mph
Length (prior to serial no. 5574)	150 inches
Standard track gauge	62 inches
Height	100 inches
Weight (prior to serial no. 5574)	
HD-10 model	20,960 pounds
HD-10W model	21,630 pounds
Injector (plunger type)	GM unit injector 6-006-155 or 6-006-155-0
Air cleaner	United
Standard track shoe width	18 inches
Number of shoes per track	
Prior to 1945 serial no. 5574	32
1945 serial no. 5574 and up	34
Rollers per side	
Prior to 1945 serial no. 5574	5
1945 serial no. 5574 and up	6
Fuel tank capacity	44 gallons
Cooling capacity	9.75 gallons
Crankcase oil capacity	13 quarts
Transmission oil capacity	6 gallons
Final drive oil capacity (each)	8 quarts
Tune-up	
Firing order	1-3-4-2
Injector timing (special tool used)	1.484 inches, plunger follower to injector body, valves open
Price	
Model HD-10	$9,250 in 1950
Model HD-10W	$9,450 in 1950
Paint	

Crawler is painted Persian Orange, yellow, or olive drab (military)

Options
Engine preheater
13.375-inch diameter by 10-inch wide belt pulley (413 and 930 rpm)
PTO assembly (192 and 430 rpm)
Crankcase and track guards
Grouser widths of 16 and 18 inches (HD-10)
Grouser widths of 16, 18, 20, 22, and 24 inches (HD-10W)
Hour meter (electric after serial no. 302)
Reverse-flow radiator fan
Cold weather starting aid

Comments
During World War II, it appears that 1,760 HD-10W models were used by the military and referred to as the Heavy Tractor M1.

Three different types of air precleaners were used on HD-10 crawlers. The first type used until 1940 serial number 515 had a dust jar and was mounted below the hood and attached to the top casting of the main air cleaner. The second type was used from serial number 515 to approximately 1146 and was stack-mounted with a removable dust jar. The final type was a stack-mounted type with a sight glass in a dome-shaped metal shell.

Several gears in the transmission were changed at 1942 serial number 1785 and up.

The standard 32-link track chain was changed to 34 links at 1945 serial number 5574 and after. Other special track lengths were available, such as the 32-link short track still available after serial number 5574 and the 33-link track chain. Special long-track versions were available with 34- and 35-link track chains. Standard track lengths used a 26.5-inch diameter track idler, while the special track versions used a 29.5-inch idler.

Model HD-10 Standard Features
62-inch track gauge
18-inch grousers
Front bumper
12-volt starter and generator with lights

Model HD-10W Standard Features
74-inch track gauge
18-inch grousers
Front bumper
12-volt starter and generator with lights

Production History (HD-10 models, 62-inch track gauge)*

Year	Beginning number
1940	2
1941	642
1942	not found
1943	not found
1944	3652
1945	not found
1946	6103
1947	6576
1948	7799
1949	8710
1950	9634
Ending serial number	10198

*The starting serial numbers for the HD-10W are not the same as the standard model in some years. The two lists for the HD-10 and HD-10W are interspersed in the same serial number run.

Production History (HD-10W models, 74-inch track gauge)

Year	Beginning number
1940	2
1941	642
1942	1446W
1943	2082W
1944	2339W
1945	4095W
1946	5964W
1947	6463W
1948	7602W
1949	8676W
1950	9631W

Weighing a little less than 6 tons, the Model HD-5 Crawler sold more than 29,000 crawlers during its 10 years of production. Introduced in 1946, this popular model was powered by a two-cylinder General Motors diesel engine.

Allis-Chalmers HD-5 Crawler (total production 29,255)

Nebraska test number	396
Serial numbers	1–29255
Location of serial numbers	rear side of steering clutch housing at upper right corner
Location of engine number	right side of block by governor
Production years	1946–1955
Total production	29,255
Engine	General Motors vertical, two-cylinder diesel (two-cycle)
Bore and stroke	4.25x5.0 inches
Rated rpm	1,800
Displacement	142 cubic inches
Compression ratio	16.0:1
Fuel	diesel
Engine ratings	
Drawbar	38.24 horsepower
PTO/belt	47.85 horsepower
Maximum pull	10,059 pounds
Speed	
All HD-5 models except HD-5G, 1954 and after	
First gear	1.46 mph
Second gear	2.44 mph
Third gear	3.30 mph
Fourth gear	3.96 mph

Fifth gear	5.47 mph
Reverse	1.99 mph

Model HD-5G (loader) 1954 and after

First gear	1.5 mph
Second gear	2.4 mph
Third gear	3.3 mph
Fourth gear	5.5 mph
Reverse (low)	2.0 mph
Reverse (high)	4.1 mph
Length (HD-5A, HD-5B)	124.875 inches
Standard track gauge (HD-5A)	44 inches
Height	60.375 inches
Weight (HD-5A)	11,815 pounds
Injector (plunger type)	GM unit injector
Air cleaner (with precleaner)	
Serial nos. 1857–1946	Donaldson (oil)
Serial nos. prior to 1857 and after 1946	United (oil)
Standard track shoe width	13 inches
Number of shoes per track	
HD-5A and HD-5B	33
HD-5F and HD-5G	37
Rollers per side	
HD-5A and HD-5B	4
HD-5F and HD-5G	5
Fuel tank capacity	37 gallons
Cooling capacity	3.75 gallons
Crankcase oil capacity	8 quarts
Transmission oil capacity	5 gallons
Final drive oil capacity (each)	3 gallons
Injector timing (special tool used)	1.484 inches, plunger follower to injector body, valves open

Price

Model HD-5A (44-inch track gauge)	$6,585 in 1955
Model HD-5B (60-inch track gauge)	$6,675 in 1955
Model HD-5F (long track)	$7,525 in 1955
Model HD-5G (loader)	$10,230 in 1953

Paint

The crawler is painted Persian Orange, yellow, or olive drab (military). The "Allis-Chalmers" hood transfers are 3x30.5 inches unless the air precleaner extension is used, then 1.75x12.75-inch transfers are used. Three 4.5x14.75-inch "Allis-Chalmers HD-5 Diesel" transfers are used with one on each side of the seat and one on the rear of the fuel tank.

Options

Four-speed forward and two-speed reverse transmission
    (This transmission standard on HD-5G at serial no. 13309 and up)
Canopy top or cab (includes canopy top and enclosures with glass)
Curtains for canopy top
Engine preheater (standard equipment prior to serial no. 4208)
Odometer (mounted at top of steering clutch housing)

Hour meter (mounted at left side of seat) and fuel oil pressure gauge
Heavy-duty oil and fuel filters (Luberfiner brand)
Rear tank and seat guard (not for crawlers with heavy-duty filters)
Louvered engine side covers
Inner and outer track guards (standard on HD-5E, HD-5F, and HD-5G)
Rear floodlight or taillight
Precleaner extension (extends precleaner 70 inches above cowl)
Exhaust deflector or rain cap
Front pull hook
Heavy radiator guard (standard on HD-5G after approx. 1951)
Heavy-duty core radiator
Pusher type fan plus grille screen (standard on HD-5G)
Radiator curtain
10- or 12-inch diameter by 8.75-inch wide belt pulley (963 rpm)
PTO assembly: regular (963 rpm) or reversible reduction (539 rpm)
PTO guard
Heavy-duty, front equalizer six-leaf spring (HD-5B and HD-5E only)
Track shoe widths of 7, 13, 15, 16, 18, and 20 inches
    (13-inch shoe maximum on HD-5A, HD-5B, or HD-5G)
Special tool kit (mounts on left fender)

Comments

Beginning approximately August 1948, the engine numbering system was changed. The early system used the prefix "271," designating two cylinders with 71 cubic inches per cylinder. After August 1948, the prefix "2A," which still denoted a two-cylinder, was used and the number sequence was restarted.

Track shoes on HD-5 crawlers before serial number 1053 came with holes spaced 9.5 inches apart for attaching demountable grousers; later models had holes spaced 7.5 inches apart and used different grousers.

An ether capsule dispenser was used for cold weather starting on HD-5 crawlers built at 1948 serial number 4208 and after. An engine air heater that burns vaporized fuel oil was used for cold weather, starting before serial number 4208, but was still optional afterwards.

An Eaton brand rotor-type fuel pump was used on HD-5 crawlers prior to engine number 271-14936 and a Barnes gear-type afterward.

Model HD-5A Standard Features
44-inch track gauge
Spring equalizer front track support (seven-leaf spring)
33-link track chain (four rollers) with 13-inch grousers
Full-width crankcase guard and front bumper
Muffler
Hinged radiator guard
12-volt Delco-Remy 1109114 starter and Guide brand lights

Model HD-5B Standard Features
60-inch track gauge
Spring equalizer front track support (seven-leaf spring)
33-link track chain (four rollers) with 13-inch grousers
Full-width crankcase guard and front bumper
Muffler

Model HD-5 Crawler

Hinged radiator guard
12-volt Delco-Remy 1109114 starter and Guide brand lights

Model HD-5E Standard Features
60-inch track gauge
Spring equalizer front track support (seven-leaf spring)
37-link track chain (five rollers) with 13-inch grousers
Full-width crankcase guard and front bumper
Muffler
Hinged radiator guard
Inner and outer track guards
12-volt Delco-Remy 1109114 starter and Guide brand lights

Model HD-5F Standard Features
60-inch track gauge
Rigid-beam front track support
37-link track chain (five rollers) with 13-inch grousers
Full-width crankcase guard and front bumper
Muffler
Hinged radiator guard
Inner and outer track guards
12-volt Delco-Remy 1109114 starter and Guide brand lights

Model HD-5G Standard Features
60-inch track gauge
Rigid-beam front track support
37-link track chain (five rollers) with 13-inch grousers
1-yard capacity front-mounted shovel (0.75 and 1.5-yard optional)
Full-width crankcase guard and front bumper
Muffler
Hinged radiator guards
Inner and outer track guards
12-volt Delco-Remy 1109114 starter and Guide brand lights

Production History (Model HD-5)

Year	Beginning number
1946	1
1947	7
1948	1358
1949	4316
1950	7499
1951	11071
1952	14290
1953	17558
1954	21837
1955	25564
Ending serial number	29255

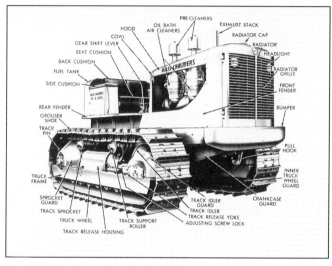

The HD-19 Crawler was introduced in 1947 as a replacement for the reliable but aging Model HD-14. With basically the same General Motors six-cylinder diesel engine, the Model HD-19 weighed almost 6 tons more than the HD-14.

Allis-Chalmers Model HD-19 Crawler (total production 2,650)

Nebraska test number	397
Serial numbers	4–2653
Location of serial number	rear face of steering clutch housing near upper right corner
Location of engine number	right side of block by governor
Production years	1947–1950
Total production	2,650
Engine	General Motors six-cylinder diesel (two-cycle)
Bore and stroke	4.25x5.0 inches
Rated rpm	1,750
Displacement	426 cubic inches
Compression ratio	16.0:1
Fuel	diesel
Engine ratings	
Drawbar	110.64 horsepower
PTO/belt	129.08 horsepower
Maximum pull	37,536 pounds
Speed (torque converter)	
Low-range	0–3.0 mph
High-range	0–7.0 mph
Reverse	0–5.5 mph

154

Length	190.75 inches
Standard track gauge	84 inches
Height (without exhaust pipe)	87.8125 inches
Weight (HD-19H)	40,395 pounds
Injector (plunger type)	GM unit injector (70 cubic millimeters)
Air cleaner	United (two units)
Standard track shoe width (HD-19H)	24 inches
Number of shoes per track (HD-19H)	37
Rollers per side (HD-19H)	6
Useable fuel tank capacity	
Prior to serial number 1123	99 gallons
Serial number 1123 and after	120 gallons
Cooling capacity	
Prior to serial number 1802	11 gallons
Serial number 1802 and after	13 gallons
Crankcase oil capacity (with filters)	5 gallons
Transmission oil capacity	9.75 gallons
Final drive oil capacity (each)	7.5 gallons
Track release housing oil capacity (each)	5.5 gallons
Tune-up	
Firing order	1-5-3-6-2-4
Injector timing (special tool used)	1.460 inches from plunger follower to injector body with valves open
Price (Model HD-19H)	$16,500 in 1950
Paint	Persian Orange or yellow

Options

22-, 24-, 26-, 28-, and 30-inch track shoes in several styles
Heavy rear fenders
Mesh grille screen
Engine side covers or side screens
Fuel tank and seat guards (Model HD-19H only)
Bottom guard group (two sections for Model HD-19H only)
Pusher plate (replaces front bumper)
Skeleton sprocket (fits serial number 704 and up)
Hour meter (Hobbs brand)
Air precleaner extensions (uses special hood)
Reverse-flow fan
20-inch diameter x 15-inch wide power pulley
Taillight or rear floodlight
Canopy with optional enclosures to make a cab with sliding doors

Comments

The HD-19H has an oscillating undercarriage with the front of the tracks supported by a five-leaf spring equalizer. The HD-19H has a 37-link track chain, making it very suitable for agricultural duties. The HD-19F has a rigid track support with a 40-link track chain, making it well suited for construction work. The HD-19G is the same as the HD-19F, but with a mounted Tractomotive brand front loader.

The standard cold weather starting aid on models built before 1948 serial number 1166 was an air heater system. The air heater used diesel fuel sprayed by a nozzle and electrically ignited to create a flame in the engine air box. At serial number 1166 and after, the air heater system became optional and the standard starting aid was ether. Encapsulated in gelatin with 7- and 17-cc sizes, the ether charges were sprayed into the air intake elbow from a special dispenser.

Prior to 1949 serial number 1352, the HD-19 crawlers had single steering brake rods and flanged air cleaner intake elbows. At serial number 1352 and after, the brake rods were compound and the air cleaner elbows had rubber boot connections.

Prior to 1949 serial number 1802, the radiator has a 30-inch diameter fan. At serial number 1802 and after, the fan was increased to a 36-inch diameter and the radiator, grille, and hood were made larger. Serial numbers 1776 and 1777 have the 36-inch fan and the larger radiator, grille, and hood.

Model HD-19H Standard Features
Twin Disc brand three-stage torque converter (runs on diesel fuel)
Hydraulic steering controls
37-link track chain with 24-inch track shoes
Spring equalizer front track support
Hinged radiator guard and full-width crankcase guard
Front bumper and pull hook
12-volt Delco-Remy 1108811 starter plus lighting equipment

Model HD-19F Standard Features
Twin Disc brand three-stage torque converter (runs on diesel fuel)
Hydraulic steering controls
40-link track chain with 24-inch track shoes
Rigid-beam front track support
Hinged radiator guard and full-width crankcase guard
Front bumper and pull hook
12-volt Delco-Remy 1108811 starter plus lighting equipment

Model HD-19G Standard Features
Mounted Tractomotive brand loader (4-yard capacity)
Twin Disc brand three-stage torque converter (runs on diesel fuel)
Hydraulic steering controls
40-link track chain with 22-inch grousers (no size option)
Rigid-beam front track support
Hinged radiator guard
Full-width crankcase guard plus front pull hook
12-volt Delco-Remy 1108811 starter plus lighting equipment

Production History (Model HD-19)

Year	Beginning number
1947	4
1948	121
1949	1196
1950	2002
Ending serial number	2653

The Model HD-9 replaced the HD-10 in 1950. During its six years of production, less than 6,000 units were built.

Allis-Chalmers Model HD-9 Crawler (total production 5,850)

Nebraska test number	463
Serial numbers	1–5850
Location of serial number	rear face of steering clutch housing, upper right corner
Location of engine number	right side of block near governor
Production years	1950–1955
Total production	5,850
Engine	General Motors four-cylinder diesel (two-cycle)
Bore and stroke	4.25x5.0 inches
Rated rpm	1,600
Displacement	284 cubic inches
Compression ratio	16.0:1
Fuel	diesel
Engine ratings	
Drawbar	67.39 horsepower
PTO/belt	79.10 horsepower
Maximum pull	19,035 pounds
Speed	
First gear	1.4 mph
Second gear	2.1 mph

Third gear	2.9 mph
Fourth gear	3.8 mph
Fifth gear	4.4 mph
Sixth gear	5.7 mph
Reverse (low)	1.6 mph
Reverse (medium)	3.5 mph
Reverse (high)	4.4 mph
Length (HD-9B)	150 inches
Standard track gauge (all HD-9 models)	74 inches
Height (without stacks)	73.125 inches
Weight (HD-9B shipping)	19,995 pounds
Injector (plunger type)	GM unit injector
Air cleaner	United
Standard track shoe width	16 inches
Number of shoes per track	
HD-9B	38
HD-9F, HD-9G	41
Rollers per side	
HD-9B	6
HD-9F, HD-9G	7
Fuel tank capacity	55 gallons
Cooling capacity	7.25 gallons
Crankcase oil capacity	16 quarts
Transmission oil capacity	6.75 gallons
Final drive oil capacity (each)	3.25 gallons
Tune-up	
Firing order	1-3-4-2
Injector timing (special tool used)	1.484 inches, plunger follower to injector body, valves open
Price	
Model HD-9B (agricultural)	$10,720 in 1955
Model HD-9F (construction)	$11,150 in 1955
Model HD-9G (loader)	$17,075 in 1955
Paint	Persian Orange or yellow

Options

Cab (all steel with safety glass)
Odometer (miles or kilometers) and hour meter (Hobbs brand)
Heavy-duty oil and fuel filters (Luberfiner brand)
Heavy fenders and bottom guards
Skeleton sprocket
Engine side screens or louvered side plates
Precleaner extension
Exhaust deflector or rain cap
Rear taillight or floodlight
Pusher-type fan
Fuel tank guard, seat guard, and radiator screen (not for HD-9G)
Engine preheater (diesel fuel torch type)
13.375-inch diameter by 10-inch wide power pulley (929 rpm)
PTO assembly (1,600 rpm)

PTO assembly (431 rpm forward and 334 rpm reverse)
PTO guard (regular or reversible reduction)
Track shoe widths of 16, 18, 20, and 22 inches in several styles

Comments

The Model HD-9B has an oscillating undercarriage with the front of the tracks being supported by a six-leaf equalizing spring, making it well suited for agricultural purposes. The HD-9B has a 38-link track chain. The HD-9F has a rigid front undercarriage support and a 41-link track chain. The HD-9F was well suited for construction use. The HD-9G is much like the HD-9F, but has a mounted Tractomotive brand front loader.

Starting with 1952 serial number 1038 and up, the shifting lock plunger rod and boot lengths were changed.

Model HD-9 Standard Features
16-inch track shoes
38-link track chain with six lower rollers
Full-width crankcase guard and hinged radiator guard
Muffler
Front bumper and pull hook
12-volt Delco-Remy 1108811 starter and Guide brand lights

Model HD-9F Standard Features
16-inch semigrouser track shoes (no options)
41-link track chain with seven lower rollers
Full-width crankcase guard and hinged radiator guard
Muffler
Front bumper and pull hook
12-volt Delco-Remy 1108811 starter and Guide brand lights

Model HD-9G Standard Features
Mounted Tractomotive brand loader (2-yard capacity)
16-inch semigrouser track shoes (no options)
41-link track chain with seven lower rollers
Full-width crankcase guard and hinged radiator guard
Muffler
Front pull hook
12-volt Delco-Remy 1108811 starter and Guide brand lights

Production History (all Model HD-9 crawlers)

Year	Beginning number
1950	1
1951	2
1952	738
1953	1883
1954	3591
1955	5209
Ending serial number	5850

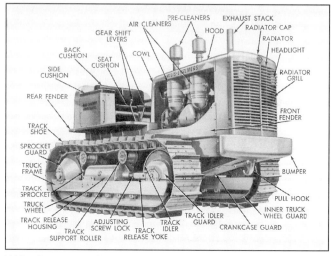

With either a six-speed constant-mesh transmission or torque converter, the 15-ton HD-15 Crawler could pull almost its own weight. Less than 4,000 units were sold during the six years of production.

Allis-Chalmers Model HD-15 Crawler (total production 3,909)

Nebraska test number	464
Serial numbers	1–3909
Location of serial number	back of steering clutch housing at top right corner and on cowl
Location of engine number	right side of block below governor control housing
Production years	1950–1955
Total production	3,909
Engine	General Motors six-cylinder diesel (two-cycle)
Bore and stroke	4.25x5.0 inches
Rated rpm	1,600
Displacement	426 cubic inches
Compression ratio	16.0:1
Fuel	diesel
Engine ratings	
Drawbar	104.37 horsepower
PTO/belt	117.68 horsepower
Maximum pull	29,400 pounds
Speed	
Six-speed constant-mesh transmission (HD-15A)	
First gear	1.39 mph
Second gear	2.09 mph

Third gear	2.97 mph
Fourth gear	3.87 mph
Fifth gear	4.46 mph
Sixth gear	5.80 mph
Reverse (low)	1.54 mph
Reverse (medium)	3.47 mph
Reverse (high)	4.51 mph
Torque converter (HD-15 C)	
Low-range	0–2.5 mph
Medium-range	0–4.3 mph
High-range	0–7.0 mph
Reverse (low-range)	0–3.2 mph
Reverse (high-range)	0–5.5 mph
Length	172.75 inches
Standard track gauge	74 inches
Height (without stacks)	84 inches
Weight (shipping)	27,500 pounds
Injector (plunger type)	GM unit injector
Air cleaner	United (two units)
Standard track shoe width	20 inches
Number of shoes per track	
Models HD-15B and HD-15C	38
Models HD-15F and HD-15G	41
Rollers per side	
Models HD-15B and HD-15C	6
Models HD-15F and HD-15G	7
Fuel tank capacity	
Six-speed models	91.5 gallons
Torque converter models	100 gallons (90 usable)
Cooling capacity	11.75 gallons
Crankcase oil capacity	20 quarts
Transmission oil capacity	
Six-speed	9.25 gallons
Torque converter (gear case)	8.0 gallons
Final drive oil capacity (each)	22 quarts
Tune-up	
Firing order	1-5-3-6-2-4
Injector timing (special tool used)	1.484 inches, plunger follower to injector body, valves open
Price	
Model HD-15A	$15,165 in 1955
Model HD-15F	$15,350 in 1955

Paint

Crawler is painted either Persian Orange or yellow with a black 3.375x30.25-inch "Allis-Chalmers Diesel" transfer on each side of the hood. Three black 5x17.75-inch transfers with "Allis-Chalmers Diesel" are used with one on the rear of the fuel tank and one on each side of the seat.

Options

Cab (all steel with safety glass)
Odometer (miles or kilometers) and hour meter (Hobbs brand)

Heavy-duty oil and fuel filters (Luberfiner brand)
Heavy-duty fenders
Skeleton track drive sprocket
Engine side plates (louvered)
Precleaner extensions (special hood used)
Exhaust deflector or rain cap
Taillight or rear floodlight
Pusher-type fan
Engine preheater (diesel fuel torch type)
18-inch diameter by 15-inch wide power pulley (693 rpm)
Straight PTO assembly (1,600 rpm)
Reversible-reduction PTO (431 rpm forward, 334 rpm reverse)
PTO guard (regular or reversible reduction)
Track shoe widths of 18, 20, 22, and 24 inches in several styles

Comments

The HD-15 was the big brother to the HD-9. The standard Model HD-15 has a six-speed manual transmission and the HD-15C has a Twin Disc brand three-stage torque converter that runs on diesel fuel from the main fuel tank. The brakes are a mechanical self-energizing type, and the grille guard is hinged for easy access.

HD-15 models using the optional heavy-duty oil and fuel filters have only a single seat, as the filter canisters are placed where the right-hand seat would be.

The HD-16 replaced the HD-15 in 1955, when Allis-Chalmers crawlers discontinued use of the General Motors diesels.

Models HD-15A and HD-15B Standard Features
38-link track chain with 20-inch shoes
Seven-leaf track equalizing spring
Full-width crankcase guard and hinged radiator guard
Drawbar (35-inch lateral adjustment)
Muffler
Front bumper and pull hook
Hydraulic steering controls (106-inch turning radius)
12-volt Delco-Remy 1108811 starter and Guide brand lights

Model HD-15C Standard Features
Same standard features as Model HD-15A, except the HD-15C has a Twin Disc brand torque converter transmission

Model HD-15F Standard Features
41-link track chain with 20-inch shoes
86-inch track gauge
Rigid-beam track equalizer
Front bumper and pull hook

Model HD-15G Standard Features
41-link track chain with 20-inch shoes
86-inch track gauge
Rigid-beam track equalizer
Tractomotive 3-yard capacity front loader (152-inch reach)

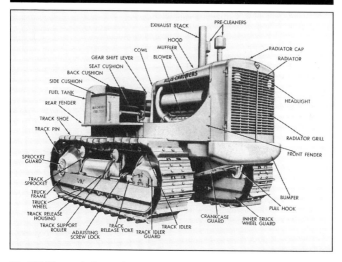

The HD-20 was the last in the series to have the General Motors diesel engine. This 21-ton machine replaced the comparable HD-19 in 1951.

Production History (HD-15 models)

Year	Beginning number
1950	1
1951	2
1952	811
1953	1858
1954	2856
1955	3685
Ending serial number	3909

Allis-Chalmers Model HD-20 Crawler (total production 3,100)

Nebraska test number	465
Serial numbers	3001–6100
Location of serial number	rear face of steering clutch housing, upper right corner
Location of engine number	right side of block by governor
Production years	1951–1954
Total production	3,100
Engine	General Motors six-cylinder diesel (two-cycle)
Bore and stroke	5x5.6 cubic inches

Rated rpm	1,700
Displacement	660.0 cubic inches
Compression ratio	18.0:1
Fuel	diesel
Engine ratings	
Drawbar	116.69 horsepower
PTO/belt	not tested
Maximum pull	41,321 pounds
Speed (two-speed torque converter)	
Low-range	0–3.0 mph
High-range	0–7.0 mph
Reverse	0–5.5 mph
Length (HD-20H)	190.75 inches
Standard track gauge	84 inches
Height (without stacks)	94.25 inches
Weight (HD-20H)	42,625 pounds
Injector (plunger type)	GM unit injector
Air cleaner	United (two units)
Standard track shoe width (HD-20H)	24 inches
Number of shoes per track (HD-20H)	37
Rollers per side	6
Fuel tank capacity (usable)	120 gallons
Cooling capacity	15 gallons
Crankcase oil capacity (with filters)	30 quarts
Transmission oil capacity	9.75 gallons
Final drive oil capacity (each)	7.5 gallons
Tune-up	
Firing order	1-5-3-6-2-4
Injector timing (special tool used)	2.425 inches, plunger follower to injector body, valves open
Price	
Model HD-20H (Agricultural)	$21,260 in 1954
Model HD-20F (Construction)	$22,575 in 1954
Model HD-20G (loader)	$33,300 in 1954

Paint

The HD-20 crawler is painted Persian Orange or yellow with a 3.75x30.5-inch black "Allis-Chalmers Diesel" transfer on either side of the hood. Three 5.5x20.25-inch transfers with "Allis-Chalmers Diesel" are used with one on the rear of the fuel tank and one on each side of the seat.

Options

Low-speed reverse (standard on later HD-20F and HD-20G models)
Cab (all steel with safety glass)
Odometer (miles or kilometers) and hour meter
Heavy-duty oil filters
Skeleton sprocket
Hood side screens or plates (HD-20H only)
Fuel tank guard, seat guard, and bottom guard (HD-20H only)
Air precleaner extensions
Exhaust rain cap
Rear taillight or floodlight

Pusher-type fan (standard on HD-20G serial no. 3404 and up)
Engine preheater (diesel fuel torch type)
20-inch diameter by 15-inch wide power pulley (400 rpm)
Track shoe widths of 22, 24, 26, and 28 inches in several styles

Comments

The HD-20H has an oscillating undercarriage with the front of the tracks supported by a five-leaf spring equalizer. The HD-20H has a 37-link track chain, making it very suitable for agricultural duties. The HD-20F has a rigid track support with a 40-link track chain, making it well suited for construction work. The HD-20G is similar to the HD-20F, but with a mounted Tractomotive brand front-end loader.

Model HD-20H Standard Features

37-link track chain with 24-inch grousers
Two-speed transmission with a Twin-Disc brand torque converter
Double seat
Front bumper
24-volt Delco-Remy 1109703 starter and Guide brand lights

Model HD-20F Standard Features

40-link track chain with 24-inch grousers (26- and 28-inch optional)
Two-speed transmission with a Twin-Disc brand torque converter
Low-speed reverse (optional prior to serial number 3964)
Single seat
Front bumper
24-volt Delco-Remy 1109703 starter and Guide brand lights

Model HD-20G Standard Features

Mounted Tractomotive brand loader (4-yard capacity)
40-link track chain with 22-inch grousers (no size option)
Two-speed transmission with a Twin-Disc brand torque converter
Low-speed reverse (optional prior to serial number 3999)
Single seat
Heavy radiator guard
24-volt Delco-Remy 1109703 starter and Guide brand lights

Production History (Model HD-20)

Year	Beginning number
1951	3001
1952	3828
1953	4923
1954	5737
Ending serial number	6100

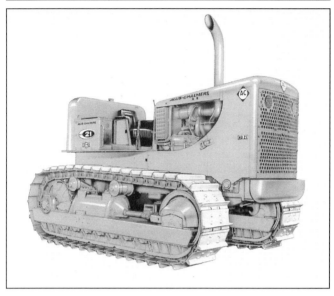

The nearly 24-ton Model HD-21 replaced the Model HD-20 in 1954. After acquiring the Buda Company in late 1953, Allis-Chalmers at last had its own diesel engines. The HD-21 carried an 884-cubic inch powerplant, giving this crawler more than 147 drawbar horsepower.

Allis-Chalmers Model HD-21 Series A Crawlers (total production 8,207)

Nebraska test number	550 and 664
Serial numbers	7001–15207
Location of serial number	rear of right final drive housing
Location of engine number	left side of block
Production years	1954–1969
Total production	8,207
Engine	Allis-Chalmers six-cylinder diesel (four-cycle)
Bore and stroke	5.25x6.5 inches
Rated rpm	
Serial numbers 7001–9000	1,800
Serial numbers 9001–15207	1,825
Model HD-21A (1963–1966)	1,875
Model HD-21P	1,900
Displacement	844 cubic inches
Compression ratio	
Serial numbers 7001–11000	13.3:1

Serial numbers 11001–15207   14.5:1
Fuel   diesel
Engine ratings
  Model HD-21AC (test no. 550 in July 1955)
    Drawbar   135.12 horsepower
    PTO/belt   not tested
    Maximum pull   40,563 pounds
  Model HD-21A (test no. 664 in September 1958)
    Drawbar   147.18
    PTO/belt   not tested
    Maximum pull   43,250 pounds
Speed (torque converter)
  Serial numbers 7001–9000
    Low-range   0– 3.0 mph
    High-range   0–7.5 mph
    Reverse   0–5.5 mph
  Serial number 9001 to year 1961 without Power-Shift
    Low-range   0–3.1 mph
    High-range   0–8.0 mph
    Reverse   0–6.0 mph
  Year 1961 and up without Power-Shift
    Low-range   0–3.3 mph
    High-range   0–6.3 mph
    Reverse   0–6.3 mph
    Optional reverse   0–4.5 mph
  Serial number 12457 and up with Power-Shift
    Low-range   0 4.1 mph
    High-range   0–7.8 mph
    Reverse (low-range)   0–3.7 mph
    Reverse (high-range)   0–7.1 mph
Length   194.75 inches
Standard track gauge   84 inches
Height (without stacks)   98.875 inches
Weight (HD-21AC)   44,725 pounds
Injector pump   Bosch
Air cleaner   Donaldson
Standard track shoe width   24 inches
Number of shoes per track
  Model HD-21 (prior to serial no.
    9001)   37
  Model HD-21 (serial no. 9001–
    15207)   40
  Model HD-21G and GC
    (loader)   42
Rollers per side
  Model HD-21 (prior to
    serial no. 9001)   6
  Model HD-21 (serial no.
    9001–15207)   7
  Model HD-21G and GC
    (loader)   8

Fuel tank capacity	130 gallons
Cooling capacity	
HD-21P	21 gallons
HD-21A	20 gallons
Crankcase oil capacity (with filters)	42 quarts
Transmission oil capacity	
HD-21P (plus torque converter and clutch)	25 gallons
HD-21A (plus steering clutches and brakes)	37 gallons
Track release spring housing oil capacity	16 quarts
Final drive oil capacity (each)	30 quarts
Price	$56,885 in 1969
Paint	

The crawler is painted Persian Orange or yellow.

Options
Cab
Hood side screens
20-inch diameter by 15-inch wide power pulley (400 rpm)
Air cleaner extensions
Lower gearing (0–2.5 mph, 0–6.0 mph, and reverse of 0–3.5 mph)

Comments
These HD-21 crawlers were unofficially referred to as the Series A after the Series B models were introduced in 1969.

The supercharger was replaced by a turbocharger in 1956, giving the HD-21 more horsepower.

In 1963, a Farr dry type cleaner replaced the Donaldson oil type air cleaner.

The HD-21GC was a loader model with a torque-converter transmission that was made from 1955 to 1968. The HD-21G loader model with a Power-Shift transmission replaced the HD-21GC in 1968 and was made until 1974.

Prior to 1960 serial number 11682, the rear motor mount was a solid L-shaped bracket. A trunnion and bracket was used afterward.

Model HD-21AC Standard Features
24-inch grousers
Front bumper and pull hook
PTO assembly (1,800 rpm)
Power steering (128-inch turning radius)
Torque converter (two-range forward, one-range reverse transmission)
16-inch three-plate master clutch (Twin Disc brand)

Model HD-21 Logger Standard Features
Heavy grille guard plus an open cab
Engine and track and full bottom guards
Front bumper and pull hook
Power steering

Model HD-21P Standard Features
Heavy-duty grille guard
Power steering
Power-shift (three-range forward, two-range reverse transmission)
40-link track chain with seven lower rollers

Model HD-21G Standard Features
4-yard capacity front-mounted loader
Heavy-duty grille
Power steering
Power-shift (two-range forward, two-range reverse transmission)
42-link track chain with eight lower rollers

Model HD-21GC Standard Features
4-yard capacity front-mounted loader
Heavy-duty grille
Power steering
Torque converter (two-range forward, one-range reverse transmission)
42-link track chain with eight lower rollers

Production History (Model HD-21A and HD-21P models)

Year	Beginning number
1954	7001
1955	7013
1956	7916
1957	9091
1958	9302
1959	11029
1960	11682
1961	11939
1962	12260
1963	12457
1964	13250
1965	13737
1966	14159
1967	14605
1968	14884
1969	15111–15207

The newer HD-21 Series B started in 1969 and ended in 1975

Allis-Chalmers offered the HD-16 in gear-drive and in torque-converter versions. From 1955 to 1970, the first series sold about 9,500 copies before being replaced by the Series B models.

Allis-Chalmers Model HD-16 Series A Crawlers (total production 9,519)

Nebraska test numbers	551 and 552
Serial numbers (all HD-16 models)	101–15521
Serial numbers (Series A)	101–9619
Location of serial number	rear of right final drive housing
Location of engine number	left side of block
Production years (all HD-16 models)	1955–1981
Production years (Series A)	1955–1970
Total production (all HD-16 models)	14,740
Total production (Series A)	9,519
Engine	Allis-Chalmers six-cylinder (four-cycle)
Bore and stroke	5.25x6.50 inches
Rated rpm	
Model HD-16AC (torque converter)	1,800
Model HD-16A (six-speed)	1,600
Displacement	844 cubic inches
Compression ratio	14.15:1
Engine ratings	
Model HD-16AC (torque converter) test no. 551	
Drawbar	101.33 horsepower

PTO	not tested
Maximum pull	29,130 pounds
Model HD-16A (six-speed) test no. 552	
Drawbar	118.69 horsepower
PTO	133.83 horsepower
Maximum pull	28,743 pounds
Model HD16-AC (torque converter)	
Low-range	0–2.5 mph
Medium-range	0–4.3 mph
High-range	0–7.2 mph
Reverse (low)	0–3.2 mph
Reverse (high)	0–5.5 mph
Model HD-16A (six-speed)	
First gear	1.39 mph
Second gear	2.09 mph
Third gear	2.97 mph
Fourth gear	3.87 mph
Fifth gear	4.46 mph
Sixth gear	5.80 mph
Reverse (low)	1.54 mph
Reverse (medium)	3.47 mph
Reverse (high)	4.51 mph
Model HD-16DP (Power-Shift)	
Low-range	0–3.5 mph
High-range	0–7.5 mph
Reverse (low)	0–3.0 mph
Reverse (high)	0–6.5 mph
Length	178.0625 inches
Standard track gauge	74 inches
Height (overall)	89.8125 inches
Weight	
Model HD-16AC	32,135 pounds
Model HD-16A	32,375 pounds
Diesel injector pump	Bosch
Air cleaner	
Prior to 1963	United (oil)
1963 and later	dry element
Standard track shoe width	20 inches
Number of shoes per track	
HD-16 models (early energy cell head)	37
HD-16 models (direct injection head)	41
HD-16GC	43
Rollers per side (nonloader models)	6 or 7
Rollers per side (Model HD-16GC)	8
Fuel tank capacity	100 gallons
Cooling capacity	17 gallons
Crankcase oil capacity	24 quarts

Transmission oil capacity	32 quarts
Final drive oil capacity (each)	22 quarts
Price	
Model HD-16A	$23,500 in 1960
Model HD-16DP (Power-Shift)	$39,035 in 1970
Paint	

The farm models were painted Persian Orange no. 2 and the construction models were usually yellow.

Options
Heavy-duty grille guard
Lighting equipment
18-inch diameter by 15-inch wide power pulley (693 rpm)
PTO: straight (430 rpm)
PTO: reversible (430 rpm forward and 355 rpm reverse)
Enclosed cab
Ether dispenser starting aid (air heater used after April 1958)
Decelerator pedal (HD-16A and HD-16D option)

Comments
The HD-16A and HD-16AC were tested at Nebraska. Many variations were made using basically the same engine. In 1958 the combustion process was changed to a direct-injection type that replaced the energy-cell type. The newer system was more reliable and delivered more power.

The mufflers prior to 1955 serial number 313 were clamped to a pipe. At serial number 313 and up, the mufflers have a flange that is bolted to the manifold with four bolts.

The track bushings' diameter was changed from 2.5 inches to 2.625 inches at 1957 serial number 2727.

An instrument light was added at 1958 serial number 3061 and up. At 1958 serial number 2921 and up, a newer throttle assembly with a decelerator pedal was used as standard equipment on Models HD-16AC, HD-16 DC, and HD-16 FC. This throttle assembly was added to the Model HD-16GC effective serial number 3067. The decelerator was optional on Models HD-16A and HD-16D.

A square-flange style oil cooler bonnet replaced a round-flange style at engine number 16-2743.

In 1970, beginning with serial number 10301, the HD-16 Series B crawlers replaced the unofficial Series A models. The Series B models had a turbocharger on their engines.

Model HD-16A Standard Features
Power steering and brakes
Constant-mesh 6-speed forward and 3-speed reverse transmission
38-link track chain with six lower rollers

Model HD-16AC Standard Features
Power steering and brakes
Torque converter (3-range forward and 2-range reverse transmission)
38-link track chain with 6 lower rollers

Model HD-16D Standard Features
Introduced in 1960
Power steering and brakes
Constant-mesh (6-speed forward and 3-speed reverse transmission)
41-link track chain with 6 lower rollers

Model HD-16DC Standard Features
Introduced in 1960
Power steering and brakes
Torque converter (3-range forward and 2-range reverse transmission)
41-link track chain with 6 lower rollers

Model HD-16DP Standard Features
Introduced in 1964
Power steering and brakes
Power-Shift (2-range forward and 2-range reverse transmission)
41-link track chain with seven lower rollers

Model HD-16GC Standard Features
Made from 1956 to 1966
Power steering and brakes
3-yard capacity front-mounted loader
Torque converter (3-range forward and 3-range reverse transmission)
43-link track chain with 8 lower rollers

Production History (HD-16 Series A models)

Year	Beginning number
1955	101
1956	1009
1957	2463
1958	2757
1959	4144
1960	4726
1961	5098
1962	5448
1963	5732
1964	6270
1965	6965
1966	7468
1967	8076
1968	8425
1969	8794
1970	9565
Ending serial number (Series A)	9619

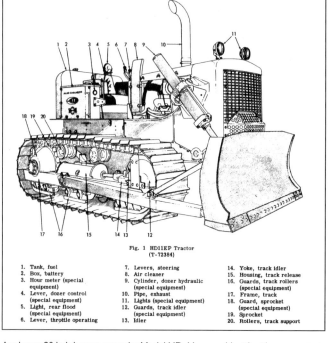

Fig. 1 HD11EP Tractor
(T-72384)

1. Tank, fuel
2. Box, battery
3. Hour meter (special equipment)
4. Lever, dozer control (special equipment)
5. Light, rear flood (special equipment)
6. Lever, throttle operating
7. Levers, steering
8. Air cleaner
9. Cylinder, dozer hydraulic (special equipment)
10. Pipe, exhaust
11. Lights (special equipment)
12. Guards, track idler (special equipment)
13. Idler
14. Yoke, track idler
15. Housing, track release
16. Guards, track rollers (special equipment)
17. Frame, track
18. Guard, sprocket (special equipment)
19. Sprocket
20. Rollers, track support

At almost 90 belt horsepower, the Model HD-11 was sold with either a constant-mesh, torque-converter, or Power-Shift transmission. The company manufactured the HD-11 from 1955 to 1970 before replacing it with the Series B in 1971.

Allis-Chalmers Model HD-11 Series A Crawlers (total production approximately 15,000)

Nebraska test number	581
Serial numbers (all HD-11 crawlers)	101–18798
Serial numbers (HD-11 Series A)	101–not found
Location of serial number	rear of right final drive housing
Location of engine number	left side of block
Production years (all HD-11 crawlers)	1955–1974
Production years (HD-11 Series A)	1955–1970
Total production (all HD-11 crawlers)	approx. 17,800
Total production (HD-11 Series A)	approx. 15,000
Engine	Allis-Chalmers six-cylinder diesel (four-cycle)
Bore and stroke	4.4375x5.5625 inches

174

Rated rpm
    HD-11 (six-speed)   1,800
    HD-11 (torque converter and
      Power-Shift)   2,050
Displacement   516 cubic inches
Compression ratio   15:1
Engine ratings (Model HD-11B, six-speed)
    Drawbar   73.80 horsepower
    PTO   89.75 horsepower
    Maximum pull   20,468 pounds
Speed
    Model HD-11 (six-speed)
      First gear   1.39 mph
      Second gear   2.10 mph
      Third gear   2.93 mph
      Fourth gear   3.77 mph
      Fifth gear   4.41 mph
      Sixth gear   5.68 mph
      Reverse (low)   1.56 mph
      Reverse (medium)   3.45 mph
      Reverse (high)   4.43 mph
    Model HD-11EC (torque converter)
      Low-range   0–2.3 mph
      Medium-range   0–4.0 mph
      High-range   0–6.9 mph
      Reverse (low)   0–2.9 mph
      Reverse (high)   0–5.1 mph
    Model HD-11EP (Power-Shift prior to 1967)
      Low-range   0–3.3 mph
      High-range   0–6.3 mph
      Reverse (low)   0–2.9 mph
      Reverse (high)   0–5.5 mph
    Model HD-11EP (Power-Shift, turbo, 1967 and up)
      Low-range   0–2.79 mph
      High-range   0–5.38 mph
      Reverse (low)   0–3.19 mph
      Reverse (high)   0–6.15 mph
Length   154 inches
Standard track gauge   74 inches
Height (overall)   84 inches
Weight (HD-11B)   22,375 pounds
Diesel injector pump
    Prior to serial no. 12201   Bosch PSB
    Serial no. 12201 and up   Roosa-Master
Air cleaner
    Prior to 1963   United (oil)
    1963 and later   dry element
Standard track shoe width   13 inches
Number of shoes per track
    Model HD-11/11B   38
    Model HD-11E, EC, EP
      (turbo models)   40

Model HD-11ES	41
Model HD-11G/ 11GC	44
Rollers per side (HD-11, 11B)	6
Rollers per side (HD-11ES)	7
Rollers per side (HD-11G, GC, F)	8
Fuel tank capacity	90 gallons
Cooling capacity	11 gallons
Crankcase oil capacity	
(plus standard filters)	15 quarts
Transmission oil capacity (six-speed)	27 quarts
Torque converter and transmission oil capacity	
(HD-11EP)	44 quarts
Final drive oil capacity (each)	13 quarts
Brakes and steering system	
oil capacity	17 gallons
Injection timing	at 36 degrees (flywheel) align
(serial no. 12201 and up)	both timing marks at pump
Price	
Model HD-11B	$18,795 in 1967
Model HD-11E	$23,250 in 1967
Model HD-11GC (loader)	$29,250 in 1967

Options

Heavy-duty grille screen
Engine air heater (fuel oil type)
13.375-inch diameter by 10-inch wide power pulley (1,045 rpm)
Swinging drawbar
Oil-type air cleaner
Heavy-duty Walker (Briggs after August, 1965) oil and fuel filters
Reverse-flow or reversible fan
Radiator guard (plain or for hydraulics)
In-line tube or armored rear tube radiator core
Engine side screens or side plates
Light-duty or heavy-duty track guards
Reinforced rear fenders
Hydraulic track adjuster
Guide brand lights (headlights and rear taillight or floodlight)
Hour meter (Stewart-Warner or Hamilton Watch Company)
Guards for fuel tank, seat, and bottom (logging)

Comments

The Model HD-11B (six-speed) was tested at Nebraska and several variations evolved soon after.

The HD-11 crawlers have double-reduction final drives and double-wrap band and drum brakes.

In 1962, the HD-11E, HD-11EC, and the Power-Shift HD-11EP were offered with a turbocharger plus improved brakes and turning clutches.

Model HD-11 crawlers prior to 1966 serial number 12201 have a 24-volt positive ground system. Models at serial number 12201 and up have a 24-volt negative ground system. The fenders, floor, and cowl were changed at the same time.

In 1971, the Series B models replaced the unofficial Series A models.

Model HD-11 and HD-11B Standard Features
Power steering
Constant-mesh (six-speed forward and three-speed reverse transmission)
38-link track chain with six lower rollers
13.5-inch, 5-plate Rockford master clutch
13.3125-inch crop clearance
Fixed drawbar
24-volt Delco-Remy 1113898 or 1113900 starter (all HD-11s)

Model HD-11E Standard Features
Power steering
Constant-mesh (six-speed forward and three-speed reverse transmission)
41-link track chain with seven lower rollers

Model HD-11S, HD-11ES, and HD-11ST Standard Features
Agricultural orientated models
Power steering
Constant-mesh transmission (HD-11S and HD11ES)
Torque-converter transmission (HD-11ST)
Light-duty grille
38-link track chain with six lower rollers (HD-11S and HD-11ST)
41-link track chain with seven lower rollers (HD-11ES)

Model HD-11EC Standard Features
Power Steering
Torque converter (three-range forward and two-range reverse transmission)
41-link track chain with seven lower rollers (prior to 1962)
40-link track chain with six lower rollers (1962 and up)

Model HD-11F Standard Features
Power steering
Torque converter (three-range forward and two-range reverse transmission)
44-link track chain with eight lower rollers

Model HD-11EP Standard Features
Power steering (111-inch turning radius)
Power-Shift (two-range forward and two-range reverse transmission)
40-link track chain with six lower rollers

Model HD-11G Standard Features
2.25-yard capacity front-mounted loader
Power steering
Constant-mesh (six-speed forward and three-speed reverse transmission)
44-link track chain with eight lower rollers

Model HD-11GC Standard Features
2.25-yard capacity front-mounted loader
Power steering
Torque converter (three-range forward and two-range reverse transmission)
44-link track chain with eight lower rollers

Production History (HD-11 Series A. Does not include Model 11E or 11EP)

Year	Beginning number
1955	101
1956	1058
1957	3255
1958	4115
1959	4768
1960	5802
1961	6448
1962	6995
1963	7870
1964	8606
1965	10533
1966	11451
1967	12251
1968	13131
1969	13657
1970	14681
Ending serial number	not found

Production History (HD-11S and HD-11ES)

Year	Beginning number
1967	1
1968	344
1969	514
1970	660
1971	1044

Allis-Chalmers sold about 25,000 HD-6s from 1955 to 1974. This 6- to 7-ton machine was a popular size for contractors as well as farmers. Versions with sliding-gear, torque-converter, or Power-Shift transmissions were produced.

Allis-Chalmers Model HD-6 Crawlers (total production 25,171)

Nebraska test number	580
Serial numbers	101–25271
Location of serial number	rear of right steering clutch housing, also on dash
Location of engine number	plate on left rear side of block
Production years	1955–1974
Total production	25,171
Engine	Allis-Chalmers four-cylinder diesel (four-cycle)
Bore and stroke	4.4375x5.5625 inches
Rated rpm	1,800
Displacement	344 cubic inches
Compression ratio	15:1
Engine ratings (HD-6B, test no. 580)	
Drawbar	49.95 horsepower
PTO	60.51 horsepower
Maximum pull	12,636 pounds
Speed	
Model HD-6 (five-speed models)	
First gear	1.46 mph
Second gear	2.44 mph

Third gear	3.30 mph
Fourth gear	3.96 mph
Fifth gear	5.47 mph
Reverse	2.00 mph
Model HD-6E (five-speed models)	
First gear	1.5 mph
Second gear	2.6 mph
Third gear	3.5 mph
Fourth gear	4.2 mph
Fifth gear	5.8 mph
Reverse	2.1 mph
Model HD-6PS and EP (torque converter)	
Low-range	0–3.0 mph
High-range	0–5.9 mph
Reverse (low)	0–2.6 mph
Reverse (high, HD-6PS)	0–4.2 mph
Reverse (high, HD-6EP)	0–5.0 mph
Length (HD-6B)	127 inches
Standard track gauge (HD-6B)	60 inches
Height (overall, HD-6B)	68.625 inches
Weight (HD-6B)	13,580 pounds
Diesel injector pump	GM
Air cleaner	
Prior to 1963	United (oil)
1963 and later	dry element
Standard track shoe width	13 inches
Number of shoes per track (standard equipment)	
Model HD-6A (prior to serial no. 5100)	33
Model HD-6A (serial no. 5100 and up)	34
Model HD-6B (prior to serial no. 5100)	33
Model HD-6B (serial no. 5100 and up)	34
Models HD-6E, HD-6EP, and HD-6PS	37
Models HD-6F and HD-6G	39
Rollers per side (standard equipment)	
Models HD-6A and HD-6B	4
Models HD-6E, HD-6EP, and HD-6PS	5
Models HD-6F and HD-6G	6
Fuel tank capacity	40 gallons
Cooling capacity	6.5 gallons
Crankcase oil capacity	10 quarts
Transmission oil capacity (five-speed)	20 quarts
Final drive oil capacity (each)	12 quarts
Tune-up	
Firing order	1-3-4-2

Injection timing
    Prior to serial no. 5100   28 degrees BTDC
    Serial no. 5100–13321   32 degrees BTDC
Price
    Model HD-6A $11,050 in 1967
    Model HD-6/6HS (dozer) $14,013 in 1967
    Model HD-6G (loader) $17,650 in 1967
Paint
The HD-6 was painted Persian Orange or yellow with a black 3.75x30.25-inch "Allis-Chalmers" transfer on each side of the hood. Black 1.75x12.75-inch "Allis-Chalmers HD-6" transfers are used at both sides of the seat and at the rear of the fuel tank.

Options
Four-speed forward and two-speed reverse (standard on HD-6G)
7-, 13-, 15-, 16-, 18-, 22-, 24-, or 28-inch track shoes
13-inch shoes maximum on 44-inch tread models or HD-6G
Track shoe styles of snow and ice, heat-treated, or cut-out
Track shoe styles of semi-, flat-, or rubber-faced
Street plates (caps over grousers)
Heavy-duty oil and fuel filters
Heavy-duty track rollers
Exhaust pipe rain shield or rain cap
10- or 12-inch diameter by 8.75-inch wide power pulley (963 rpm)
963-rpm PTO assembly or 539-rpm reversible reduction
Special radiator with armored tubes at rear of core
Pusher-type fan (standard on HD-6G)
Engine air heater (fuel oil type)
Engine side plates and bottom guards (logging)
Heavy-duty track, radiator, and fuel tank guards
Air precleaner extension tube and bracing
Taillight or floodlight (rear)
Odometer (miles or kilometers)
Hour meter (runs with an oil pressure sensor)

Comments
The HD-6 with the Allis-Chalmers diesel engine was a direct replacement for the earlier HD-5 with the General Motors diesel. The HD-6A and HD-6B were popular for agricultural uses, while longer track versions were better suited for industrial purposes.

The engine numbering system was changed in approximately March 1957. The five-digit numbering system was change to have a prefix "6-" with the number. The numbering system started a new series of engine numbers beginning with 6-7101.

Effective on Model HD-6G at serial number 1697 and other HD-6 models at serial number 3006, the Rockford clutch was replaced by an Auburn clutch. Both brands of clutches use ceramic friction discs.

The HD-6 crawlers came standard with an ether dispenser system for cold weather starting.

Model HD-6A Standard Features

Energy-cell head changed to direct-injection in 1963
Light radiator guard
44-inch track gauge
Five-leaf track equalizer spring
33 track shoes per side (prior to serial no. 5100)
34 track shoes per side (serial no. 5100 and up)
13-inch track shoes
Five-speed sliding-gear transmission
Delco-Remy 1109861 starter (on all HD-6 versions)

Model HD-6B Standard Features

Energy cell head changed to direct injection in 1963
Light radiator guard
60-inch track gauge
Five-leaf track equalizer spring
33 track shoes per side (prior to serial no. 5100)
34 track shoes per side (serial no. 5100 and up)
13-inch track shoes
Five-speed sliding-gear transmission

Model HD-6E Standard Features

Energy cell head changed to direct injection in 1963
Light radiator guard
60-inch track gauge
Five-leaf track equalizer spring
37 track shoes per side (13-inch shoes)
Five-speed sliding-gear transmission
Power steering

Model HD-6F Standard Features

Light radiator guard
60-inch track gauge
Rigid-beam track support
39 track shoes per side (13-inch shoes)
Five-speed sliding-gear transmission

Model HD-6PS Standard Features

Energy-cell head
Light radiator guard
60-inch track gauge
37 track shoes per side (13-inch shoes)
Torque converter with Power-Shift

Model HD-6EP Standard Features

Direct-injection head
Light radiator guard
60-inch track gauge
37 track shoes per side (13-inch shoes)
Torque converter with Power-Shift

Model HD-6G Standard Features

1.5-yard front-mounted Tractomotive loader
Heavy wrap-around radiator guard
60-inch track gauge
Rigid-beam track support
39 track shoes per side (13-inch shoes)
Four-speed sliding-gear transmission (1.5, 2.4, 3.3, 5.5 mph)
Two reverse gears

Production History (HD-6 crawler models)

Year	Beginning number
1955	101
1956	1147
1957	6466
1958	7948
1959	10054
1960	12506
1961	13777
1962	14898
1963	16042
1964	17105
1965	18189
1966	19401
1967	20201
1968	20809
1969	21432
1970	22272
1971	23355
1972	24012
1973	24672
1974	25012
Ending serial number	25271

Allis-Chalmers converted the popular D-15 farm tractor into two crawler versions, the H-3 and HD-3 models. Because they used the same gas and diesel engines as the D-15, parts accessibility for these crawlers were readily available, making them a popular choice for customers.

Allis-Chalmers Model H-3 and HD-3 Crawlers (total production approximately 8,243)

Nebraska test numbers	793 and 794
Serial numbers	1001–9949
Location of serial number	left front side of torque housing
Location of engine number	left side of block
Production years	1960–1968
Total production	8,243
Engine	Allis-Chalmers four-cylinder, I-head
Bore and stroke	
Model H-3 prior to serial no. 6001	3.500x3.875 inches
Model H-3 serial no. 6001 and up	3.625x3.875 inches
Model HD-3 (diesel)	3.562x4.375 inches
Rated rpm	
Model H-3 prior to serial no. 8698	1,650
Model H-3 serial no. 8698 and up	1,800
Model HD-3 prior to serial no. 8694	1,650
Model HD-3 serial number 8694 and up	1,800
Displacement	
Model H-3 prior to serial no. 6001	149 cubic inches
Model H-3 serial no. 6001 and up	160 cubic inches
Model HD-3	175 cubic inches

Compression ratio
- H-3 prior to serial no. 6001 — 7.75:1
- H-3 serial no. 6001 and up — 8.00:1
- HD-3 — 15.5:1

Fuel
- H-3 — gasoline
- HD-3 — diesel

Engine ratings (1961)
- Model H-3 (test no. 793)
  - Drawbar — 25.48 horsepower
  - PTO — 32.11 horsepower
  - Maximum pull — 7,893 pounds
- Model HD-3 (test no. 794)
  - Drawbar — 26.17 horsepower
  - PTO — 32.53 horsepower
  - Maximum pull — 8,207 pounds

Speed (H-3 and HD-3 with Shuttle Clutch)
- First gear — 1.3 mph
- Second gear — 2.0 mph
- Third gear — 2.9 mph
- Fourth gear — 4.9 mph
- Reverse (first) — 1.3 mph
- Reverse (second) — 2.0 mph
- Reverse (third) — 2.9 mph
- Reverse (fourth) — 4.9 mph

Length — 108.75 inches
Standard track gauge — 48 inches
Height (overall) — 71.6875 inches
Height (to top of hood) — 48.3125 inches
Weight
- Model H-3 — 7,395 pounds
- Model HD-3 — 7,645 pounds
Carburetor — Marvel-Schebler TSX815, TSX844, or TSX869
Diesel injector pump — Roosa-Master
Ignition — Delco-Remy 1112607
Air cleaner
- Prior to serial no. 6001 — Donaldson (oil)
- Serial no. 6001 and up — dry element
Standard track shoe width — 10 inches
Number of shoes per track — 34
Rollers per side — 4
Fuel tank capacity — 14 gallons
Cooling capacity — 9 quarts
Transmission oil capacity — 14.5 quarts
Final drive oil capacity (each) — 6.7 quarts
Hydraulic oil capacity (11.5 gpm) — 16.5 quarts
Tune-up
  See D-15 Series I and Series II tune-up sections
Price
- Model H-3 — $6,269 in 1967
- Model HD-3 — $6,914 in 1967

Model HD-3 (with six-way dozer blade)	$8,248 in 1967
Model HD-3 (with 0.75-yard front loader)	$8,804 in 1967

Paint

Agricultural models were painted Persian Orange no. 2 with a cream-colored grille. The industrial models were painted yellow.

Options

Five-roller track frame
Track shoe widths of 7, 10, 12, and 14 inches in several styles
Power-Director (two-range speed control)
PTO assembly (540 rpm)
10-inch diameter by 6-inch wide belt pulley (950 rpm)
Three-point hitch (category 2)
Three-spool hydraulic valve
15-gpm Webster hydraulic pump (early dozer)
25-gpm Webster hydraulic pump (early loader)
Bottom pan guard and track guards or heavy-duty grille
Headlights

Comments

The H-3 and HD-3 models were built on the popular D-15 tractor chassis. The undercarriage was built at the Springfield factory.

A crawler called the HD-3 was built in 1942, but was a completely different model. Only 28 of these crawlers were made using a General Motors 2-71 engine and weighing a little over 3.5 tons. This crawler was offered in a 40- or 50-inch track gauge. All data in this section is based on the later H-3 and HD-3 with the Allis-Chalmers engines.

Model H-3 and HD-3 Standard Features

Gasoline engine (H-3) or diesel engine (HD-3)
Engine-speed PTO
Shuttle clutch (reverser)
11.5-gpm hydraulic pump and one-spool valve (late models)

Production History (H-3 and HD-3 crawlers)

Year	Beginning number
1960	1001
1961	1250
1962	3199
1963	6001
1964	6945
1965	7890
1966	8856
1967 (last year of Model H-3)	9483
1968	9700
Ending serial number	9949

Paint Suggestions

The following paint formulas are close to original colors. Any recommendations in this book are made without any guarantee on the part of the author or publisher. One should compare paint company samples before committing to a color.

Allis Dark Green (1914–1928)
Martin-Senour   99L-11511
TISCO   TP380

Allis Red (for wheels 1914–1929)
Martin-Senour   99N-4359

Persian Orange (1929–1960)
PPG   DAR 60080
Martin-Senour   90R-3723
TISCO   TP280

Persian Orange no. 2 (1960–1977)
DuPont   29047
PPG   DAR 60396

Allis Cream (1960–1977)
DuPont   29049
TISCO   TP270

Allis Yellow
DuPont   Dulux 421

Rumely Green (prior to 1926)
Martin Senour   99L-2599
DuPont   Dulux 24166

Rumely Blue (1926 to 1931)
DuPont   Dulux 71939

Decimal Equivalents
(fractions to decimals)

1/64	0.015625
1/32	0.03125
1/16	0.0625
1/8	0.125
3/16	0.1875
1/4	0.25
5/16	0.3125
1/3	0.333
3/8	0.375
7/16	0.4375
1/2	0.50
9/16	0.5625
5/8	0.625
2/3	0.667
11/16	0.6875
3/4	0.75
13/16	0.8125
7/8	0.875
15/16	0.9375

Recommended Books

Gray, R.B. *Agricultural Tractor 1855–1950*. St. Joseph, Michigan: American Society of Agricultural Engineers, 1980.

Huxley, Bill. *Allis-Chalmers Agricultural Machinery*. London: Osprey Publishing, 1988.

King, Alan C. *Allis-Chalmers an Informal History, 1918–1960*. Delaware, Ohio: Independent Print Shop Company, 1989.

Mills, Robert. *Implement and Tractor Reflections on 100 Years of Farm Equipment*. Overland Park, Kansas: Intertec Publishing Corporation, 1986.

Morland, Andrew, and Peter Henshaw. *Allis-Chalmers Tractors*. Osceola, Wisconsin: MBI Publishing Company, 1997.

Swinford, Norm. *Allis-Chalmers Construction Machinery and Industrial Equipment*. Osceola, Wisconsin: MBI Publishing Company, 1998.

Swinford, Norm. *Allis-Chalmers Farm Equipment*. St. Joseph, Michigan: ASAE, 1994.

Swinford, Norm. *Guide to Allis-Chalmers Farm Tractors*. St. Joseph, Michigan: ASAE, 1996.

Wendel, C. H. *Allis-Chalmers Story*. Osceola, Wisconsin: MBI Publishing Company, 1988.

Wendel, C. H. (Photography by Andrew Morland). *Allis-Chalmers Tractors*. Osceola, Wisconsin: MBI Publishing Company, 1992.

Wendel, C. H. *Nebraska Tractor Tests Since 1920*. Osceola, Wisconsin: MBI Publishing Company, 1993.

Recommended Magazines

Antique Power
Circulation Department
P.O. Box 500
Missouri City, TX 77459
(800) 310-7047

Belt Pulley
P.O. Box 83
Nokomis, IL 62075
(217) 563-2612

Engineers and Engines
2240 Oak Leaf St.
P.O. Box 2757
Joliet, IL 60434-2757
(815) 741-2240

Gas Engine
P.O. Box 328
Lancaster, PA 17608
(717) 392-0733

Old Allis News
10925 Love Road
Bellevue, MI 49021
(616) 763-9770

Index